After-School Crafts

BARBARA L. DONDIEGO
Illustrations by JACQUELINE CAWLEY

TAB TAB BOOKS
Blue Ridge Summit, PA

NOTICES
Elmer's Glue-All®
Pringle's Potato Crisps®
Styrofoam®

Borden Inc.
Procter & Gamble
Dow Chemical Corp.

FIRST EDITION
FIRST PRINTING

© 1992 by **TAB Books**.
TAB Books is a division of McGraw-Hill, Inc.

Library of Congress Cataloging-in-Publication Data

Dondiego, Barbara L.
   After-school crafts / by Barbara L. Dondiego : illustrations by
Jacqueline Cawley.
      p.   cm.
   Includes index.
   Summary: Presents craft ideas and recipes, including how to make
juice can animal banks, papier-mâché masks, tissue paper flowers,
egg crafts, posterboard projects, and chocolate raisin bars.
   ISBN 0-8306-3869-5 (pbk.)
   1. Handicraft—Juvenile literature. [1. Handicraft.]
I. Cawley, Jacqueline, ill. II. Title.
TT160.D66 1992
745.5—dc20
                         92-13285
                            CIP
                            AC

TAB Books offers software for sale. For information and a catalog, please contact
TAB Software Department, Blue Ridge Summit, PA 17294-0850.

Acquisitions Editor: Kim Tabor
Editor: Carol Sorgen
Director of Production: Katherine G. Brown
Book Design: Jaclyn J. Boone
Cover Design: Denny Bond, East Petersburg, PA
Cover Photograph: Thompson Photography, Baltimore, MD
                                               TAB1

After-School Crafts

To Amanda

Contents

Acknowledgments

A special thank-you goes to my family for putting up with a wife/mom who covers the dining table with dinosaurs, saves milk lids, and dyes the cat blue. Thank you also to Chris and David Persson for allowing me to teach classes in their store, *The School Box*.

Preface

Two thousand years ago young shepherds fashioned flutes from tree branches. Two hundred years ago little girls created dolls from dried apples and cornhusks, and little boys whittled whistles that really worked. Thirty years ago boys bought kits to make small airplanes, boats, and cars, and girls made clothespin dolls with extensive wardrobes. Children have always enjoyed making things with their hands, but today they have little opportunity to do so. Parents are busy, craft kits are expensive, teachers have to focus on lesson plans instead of art projects, and the television set has become the nation's babysitter.

After-School Crafts was written to help children invent their own craft kits from items that are easy to find. It encourages recycling by using household items that are usually thrown away. With a little bit of adult help for short periods of time, any child from six to twelve years of age can make the crafts in this book. Believe me when I say that their imagination and creative abilities will flourish, and that television will soon lose some of its magic appeal.

How to Use this Book

The purpose of this book is to provide enjoyable activities for children to do after school. Parents and children can sit down together the night before and go through the book, choosing a craft activity for the following afternoon. Then you can all go over the instructions, prepare the materials, and read the introduction that begins each craft.

Before making the craft,

- Cover your work area with newspaper and wear an old shirt over your clothes.
- Use tracing paper to copy the patterns you need.
- Use Elmer's Glue-All to glue your crafts. The Borden Company that makes Glue-All does not pay me to say this. I just feel that their glue dries the fastest and sticks the best.
- Follow the directions. Ask an adult to help if you don't understand.

This is a book of ideas. Make each craft the way you want it to look. After you make the Biplane, for instance, make another one with wings that you invent. Decorate the American Eagle with your own designs. These are your projects.

Introduction

After-School Crafts is packed with fun and creative ideas for children ages 6 to 12.

It's a perfect book for children who love to make things. It has nearly 50 ideas, including five nifty recipes, and is a companion for the author's earlier books, *Crafts for Kids: A Month-by-Month Idea Book, 2nd Edition,* and *Year-round Crafts for Kids*. It shows a child—or an adult who works with school-age children—how to be creative with everyday items such as juice cans, coffee filters, and eggshells. The children can transform these found objects into animal banks, colorful mosaics, and fragrant sachets. The activities are also terrific ideas for school projects—try a Stegosaurus Dinosaur or a Clay Diorama, for example, to tie in with a unit on prehistoric times.

Most important, the crafts encourage children to become more creative. Their imaginations bloom as they learn to make a biplane from a toilet paper roll or a sand painting with dry cereal. By following the instructions, children will learn construction techniques that let them imagine, design, and create in new ways, yet with common, inexpensive materials.

This book is easy to use. Each craft includes a list of materials needed and step-by-step directions. Full-sized patterns are easy to trace. Realistic illustrations by Chicago artist Jacqueline Cawley let the child see exactly how the finished project will look. Helpful hints, called *woolie-pullies*, are found throughout the book to make crafts easier, neater, and less expensive.

For children to be creative they need three things: materials with which to create, the freedom of time and opportunity, and some basic ideas. The materials for these crafts are inexpensive and easy to find. After school, weekends, and vacations are perfect times for creativity. *After-School Crafts* is full of ideas and techniques to give young imaginations a head start. So have your children turn off the television set, cover the table with newspaper, roll up their sleeves, and have some fun!

I

Cylinder Crafts

Design a dragon with fire in his head!
Create a Stegosaurus Dinosaur instead.
Glue a cat and mouse friend to sit by
your bed.
You can make these things;
This book shows you how.
Get some paper towel rolls.
We'll start right now!

FIRE-BREATHING DRAGON

The fire-breathing dragon is a make-believe monster that has been in stories for thousands of years. Some dragons are good and some are evil. This dragon's fire is made of bright tissue paper.

Materials List

- 3-by-5-inch squares of red, orange, and yellow tissue paper
- Paper towel roll
- Ruler
- Scissors
- Pencil
- Elmer's Glue-All
- Posterboard
- Markers
- Notebook reinforcers

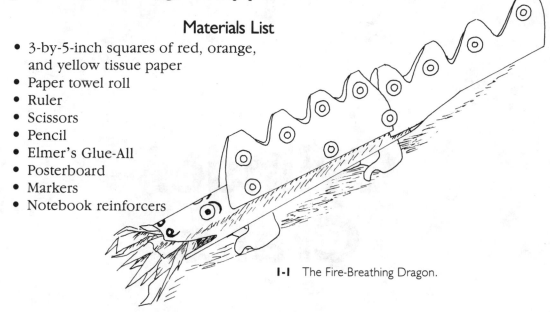

1-1 The Fire-Breathing Dragon.

Directions

1. To make the cylinder body, cut a 9-by-11-inch rectangle from construction paper. Spread glue on it. Wrap it around the paper towel roll.

2. To make the fin and the tail, copy the pattern in FIG. 1-2. Fold construction paper in half, and lay the top of the pattern on the fold. Trace and cut out. Repeat this step with another piece of paper. Glue one end of the tail on the body (FIG. 1-3). Then put glue inside the rest of the tail and press it together. Spread glue along the inside bottom edges of the fin. Glue the fin to both sides of the body (FIG. 1-4). Cut out a triangle mouth. This dragon has a mouth $2^1/2$ inches long and $1^1/4$ inches wide.

3. To make the legs, copy the pattern in FIG. 1-2. Trace two sets of legs and two props onto posterboard. Cut them out. Fold them on the dotted lines. Color them. Glue one set of legs in front, behind the mouth. Glue the other set in back. Glue a prop between each set of legs to make them stronger (FIG. 1-5).

4. Decorate the dragon with notebook reinforcers. Use two reinforcers for the dragon's eyes and color the centers black. Draw nostrils and eyebrows.

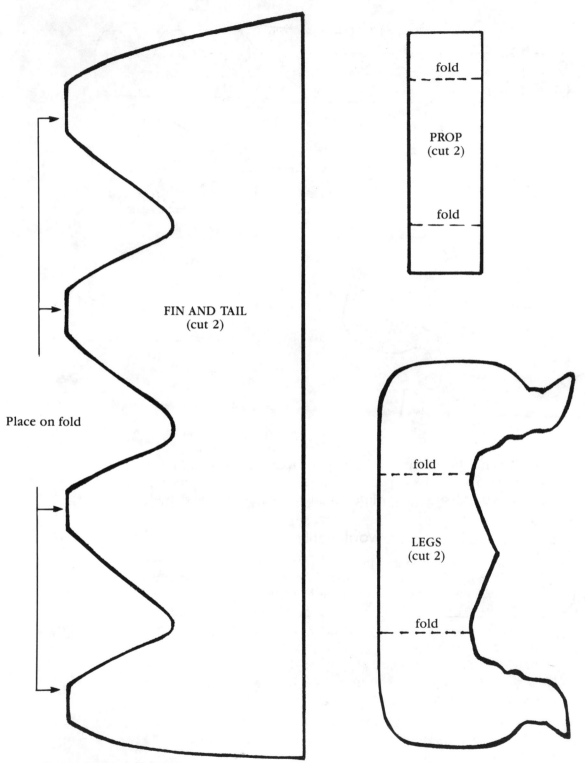

fold

PROP
(cut 2)

fold

FIN AND TAIL
(cut 2)

Place on fold

fold

LEGS
(cut 2)

fold

1-2 The patterns for the Fire-Breathing Dragon.

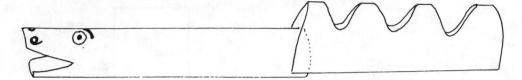

1-3 Glue one end of the tail on the body.

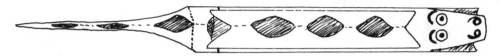

1-4 Glue the fin to both sides of the body.

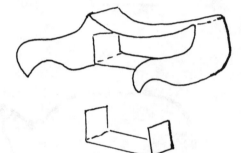

1-5 Glue a prop between each set of legs.

5. To make the "fire," spread some glue inside the dragon's mouth. Put the center of each tissue paper in the mouth so the corners are sticking out. Snip the tissue into pointed triangles that look like flames.

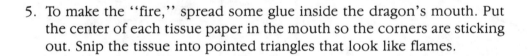

──────────── **woolie-pullie** ────────────

Use a milk bottle lid to hold glue. You can dip craft pieces in the glue, or you can use your finger to dip into the glue. Throw away the lid or set it aside and let the glue dry in it. You can put more glue in it the next time you make a craft.

DIMETRODON DINOSAUR

The Dimetrodon lived in North America 280 million years ago. It was over 11 feet long with a large back fin that kept it cool. It was a ferocious meat-eater with claws and sharp teeth. Scientists don't know what color it was because only fossil bones are left.

Materials List

- Paper towel roll
- Construction paper
- Ruler
- Scissors
- Pencil
- Elmer's Glue-All
- Water-base markers
- Posterboard

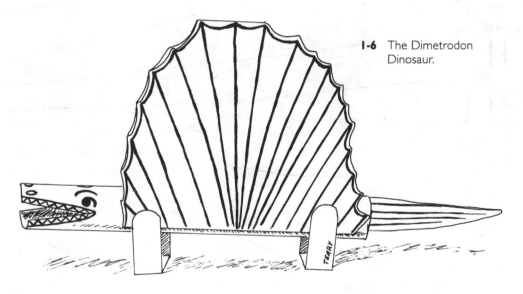

1-6 The Dimetrodon Dinosaur.

Directions

1. To make the cylinder body, cut a 9-by-11-inch rectangle from construction paper. Spread glue on it. Wrap it around the paper towel roll.

2. To make the fin, copy the pattern in FIG. 1-7. Fold a sheet of construction paper in half. Lay the top of the pattern on the fold. Trace and cut out. Outline the fin with a black marker. Draw spines on it.

3. Spread glue along the inside bottom edges of the fin. Glue the fin on each side of the body (FIG. 1-6). Cut out a triangle mouth. This Dimetrodon has a mouth 2³/₄ inches long and 1 inch wide.

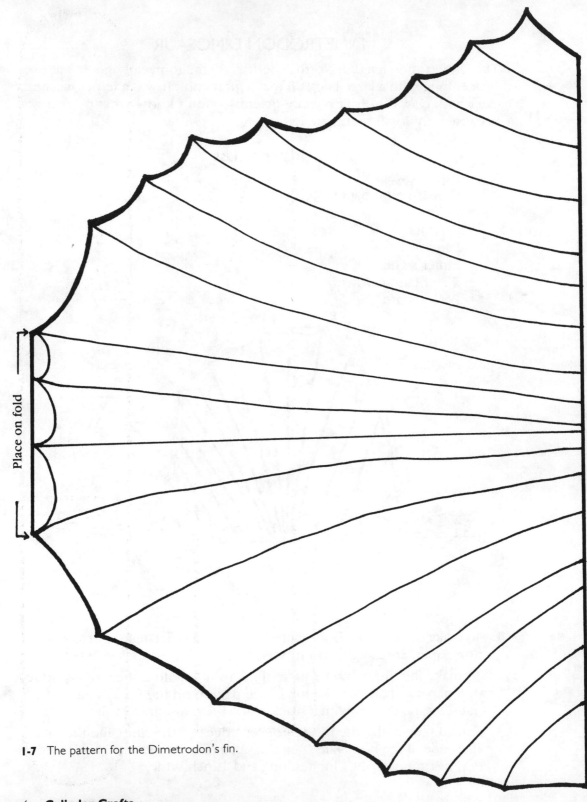

Place on fold

I-7 The pattern for the Dimetrodon's fin.

I-8 The patterns for the Dimetrodon's tail and legs.

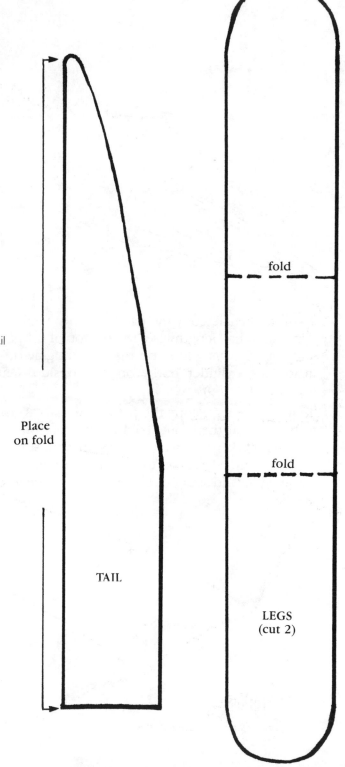

Place
on fold

fold

fold

TAIL

LEGS
(cut 2)

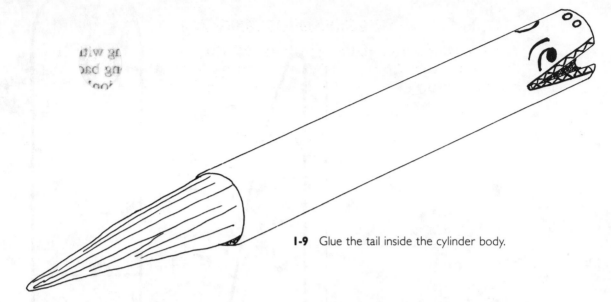

1-9 Glue the tail inside the cylinder body.

4. To make the tail, copy the pattern in FIG. 1-8. Fold a piece of paper 3 by 7 inches in half lengthwise. Lay the top of the pattern on the fold. Trace and cut out. Draw lines on the tail. Put glue on the wide end. Glue it inside the cylinder body, on the topside. Glue the tip of the tail together (FIG. 1-9).

5. To make the legs, copy the pattern in FIG. 1-8. Trace two legs onto posterboard. Cut them out. Fold them up on the dotted lines. Use light-colored markers to color the legs on both sides. Use a black marker to draw feet and claws. Set the Dimetrodon up while you glue his legs on so he will stand straight. Lay him on his side to dry.

STEGOSAURUS DINOSAUR

The Stegosaurus lived 190 million years ago. It was 20 feet long with large bony plates on its back. It walked on short front legs and long back legs and ate soft plants. Its head and brain were very small. We don't know what color it was.

Materials List

- Paper towel roll
- Construction paper
- Ruler
- Scissors
- Pencil
- Elmer's Glue-All
- Styrofoam egg carton
- Paper punch
- Posterboard

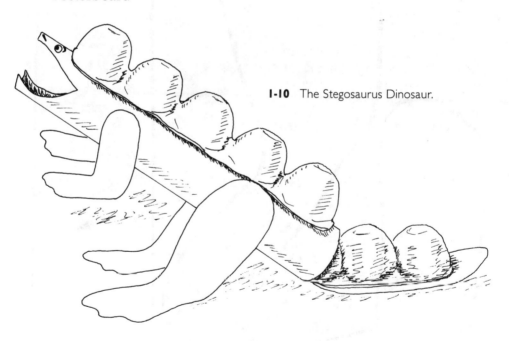

I-10 The Stegosaurus Dinosaur.

Directions

1. To make the cylinder body, cut a 9-by-11-inch rectangle from construction paper. Spread glue on it. Wrap it around the paper towel roll.

2. To make the tail, copy the pattern in FIG. 1-11. Fold a piece of construction paper in half. Lay the top of the pattern on the fold. Trace and cut

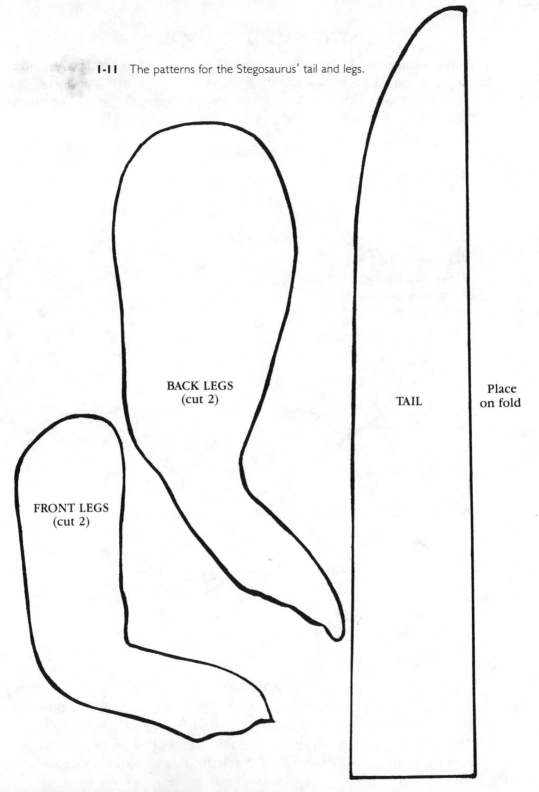

1-11 The patterns for the Stegosaurus' tail and legs.

BACK LEGS
(cut 2)

FRONT LEGS
(cut 2)

TAIL

Place
on fold

out. Cut the lid off the egg carton. Cut the egg cups into two strips of six cups each. Trim the edges. Cut off three cups (leave them stuck together) and put glue on the bottom edges. Lay them on the tail, beginning at the wide end. Let them dry.

3. Cut a mouth in one end of the body. This Stegosaurus has a mouth 2 inches long and 1$\frac{1}{2}$ inches wide.

4. Cut off five egg cups in a strip. Put glue on the bottom edges. Press them onto the back of the dinosaur. Hold them in place for a little while, or tape them in place until the glue dries.

5. To make legs, copy the patterns in FIG. 1-11. Trace the legs onto poster-board. Cut out. Glue them onto the body (FIG. 1-10).

6. To put on the tail, force the egg cup at the wide end of the tail into the open end of the cylinder body. It will stick there, leaving a two-cup tail (FIG. 1-12). Add paper-punch eyes.

1-12 To put on the tail, force the egg cup into the cylinder body.

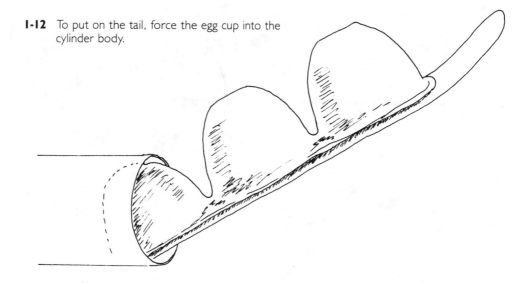

BIPLANE

In 1903 Orville and Wilbur Wright invented and flew the first airplane. It was called a biplane. Biplanes are easy to steer at slow speeds. They're used to dust chemicals on crops and to do aerobatics which are stunts in the air.

Materials List

- Toilet paper roll
- Construction paper
- Posterboard
- Ruler
- Pencil
- Scissors
- Elmer's Glue-All
- Straight pin
- Markers, stars, flag stickers

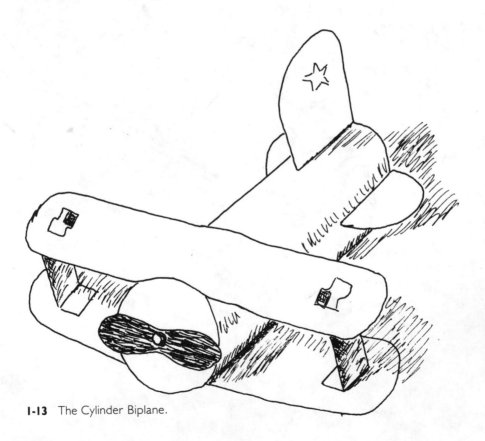

1-13 The Cylinder Biplane.

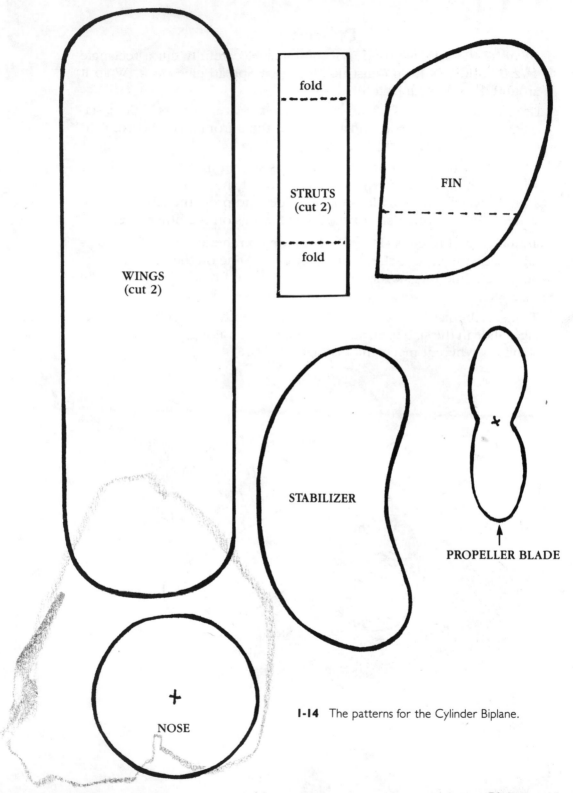

WINGS
(cut 2)

STRUTS
(cut 2)

fold

fold

FIN

STABILIZER

PROPELLER BLADE

NOSE

1-14 The patterns for the Cylinder Biplane.

Directions

1. To make the fuselage (body) of the biplane, carefully cut a rectangle 4$\frac{1}{2}$ by 6 inches from construction paper. Spread glue on it. Wrap it around the toilet paper roll.

2. Use the patterns in FIG.1-14 to cut out two wings and struts, a fin, a stabilizer, a propeller blade, and a nose. Cut them from posterboard. Fold the struts on the dotted lines.

3. Glue one wing on top of the fuselage, as shown in FIG. 1-15, and one wing on the bottom. Put glue on the tabs of the two struts. Put one strut between the two wings on one side, and press the tabs onto the wings. Glue the other strut between the wings on the other side.

4. To insert the fin, cut a slit 1$\frac{3}{4}$ inches long on the top rear of the fuselage. Slide the fin into the slit. Use the dotted line on the fin as a guide. Squeeze a line of glue along both sides of the fin where it meets the fuselage.

5. To insert the stabilizer, cut a 1$\frac{1}{2}$-inch slit on both sides of the rear fuselage. Slide in the stabilizer. Squeeze a line of glue along both sides of the stabilizer where it meets the fuselage (FIG. 1-16).

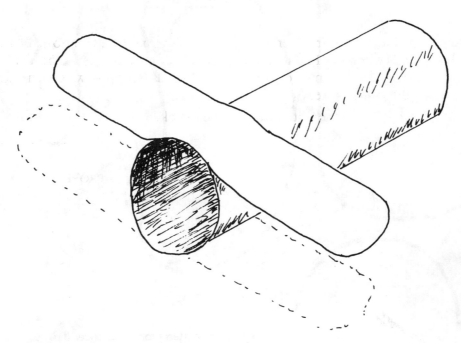

1-15 Glue one wing on top of the fuselage.

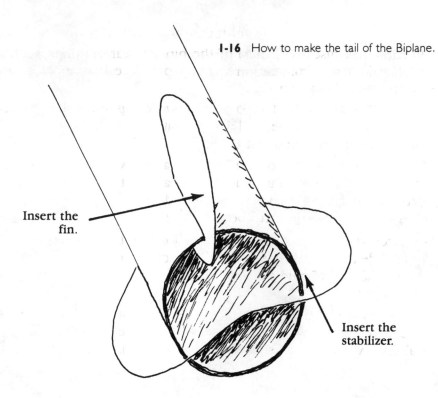

Insert the fin.

Insert the stabilizer.

6. Spread glue on the front end of the cylinder. Press on the nose. Color the propeller blade. Put a straight pin through the center of the blade, then through the center of the nose. Add a dab of glue where the pin enters the nose, to keep it from falling out.

7. Decorate the biplane with stars and flag stickers.

ALLIE CAT

Toilet paper roll cylinders can be turned into all sorts of things, such as this cute Allie Cat. Use your creation as a toy, a knicknack, or a place card at a party.

Materials List

- Black fine-line marker or black pen
- Toilet paper roll
- White construction paper
- Crayons
- Ruler
- Scissors
- Elmer's Glue-All
- Paper punch

1-17 Allie Cat.

Directions

1. Cut the toilet paper roll in half by pressing it shut in the middle and cutting straight across. Be careful with sharp scissors! Measure and cut a rectangle $2\frac{1}{4}$ by 6 inches from white construction paper. Spread glue on it. Wrap it around the cylinder.

2. Use the patterns in FIG. 1-18 to trace and cut out a head, two front paws, two back paws, and a tail. Make these from white construction paper.

3. Draw a face on the head, using a fine-line marker or pen. Add a paper-punch nose. Draw tiny claws on the feet.

4. Dot glue around one edge of the cylinder. Stick on the front paws first, then the head. Glue the back paws on the sides, near the back of the cylinder.

5. To glue on the tail, pretend the back of the cat is a clock. Dot glue on the cylinder edge at 6 o'clock and at 12 o'clock. Lay the tail on the glue dots (FIG.1-19).

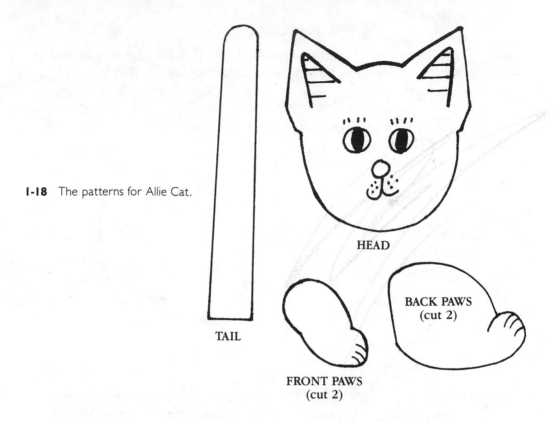

1-18 The patterns for Allie Cat.

TAIL

HEAD

FRONT PAWS
(cut 2)

BACK PAWS
(cut 2)

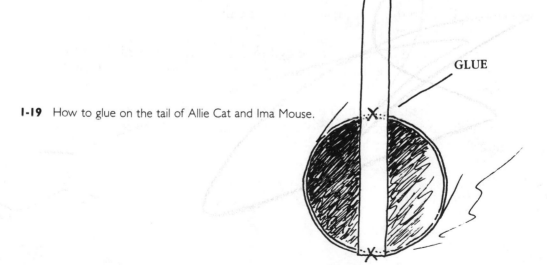

1-19 How to glue on the tail of Allie Cat and Ima Mouse.

GLUE

IMA MOUSE

Toilet paper roll cylinders, from which Ima Mouse is made, are sturdy and plentiful. They are very good material for crafts. Best of all, they're free!

Materials List

- Black fine-line marker or black pen
- Toilet paper roll
- White construction paper
- Crayons
- Ruler
- Scissors
- Elmer's Glue-All
- Paper punch

1-20 Ima Mouse.

Directions

1. Cut the toilet paper roll in half by pressing it shut in the middle and cutting straight across. Measure and cut a rectangle 2^1/$_4$ by 6 inches from white construction paper. Spread glue on it. Wrap it around the cylinder.

2. Use the patterns in FIG. 1-21 to trace and cut out a head, two front paws, two back paws, and a tail. Make these from white construction paper.

3. Draw a face on the head, using a fine-line marker or pen. Add a paper-punch nose. Draw tiny claws on the feet.

4. Dot glue around one edge of the cylinder. Stick on the front paws first, then the head. Glue the back paws on the sides, near the back of the cylinder.

5. To glue on the tail, pretend the back of the mouse is a clock. Dot glue on the cylinder edge at 6 o'clock and at 12 o'clock. Lay the tail on the glue dots (FIG. 1-19).

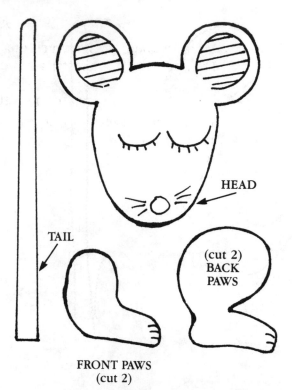

1-21 The patterns for Ima Mouse.

HEAD

TAIL

(cut 2)
BACK
PAWS

FRONT PAWS
(cut 2)

2

Juice Can Animal Banks

Drink some juice and save some cash.
Four animal banks will hold it tight!
Make a Panda Bank to guard it for you,
Or a steer, snake, and lion;
They're all fun to do!

For a neat papier-mâché project, each child can use a small, disposable Styrofoam bowl to hold her own flour-water paste. An adult can fill the bowls with more paste as needed, and the children can stay at their workplace.

GIANT PANDA BANK

The Giant Panda is rare. He lives in China and Tibet, and his favorite food is bamboo. He can grow to be five feet tall and weigh 350 pounds. Although he looks like a bear, he's probably a large cousin of the raccoon!

Materials List

- 12-ounce juice can
- White, black, and brown construction paper
- Black marker
- Posterboard
- Ruler
- Scissors
- Elmer's Glue-All
- Paper punch
- Popsicle stick

2-1 The Giant Panda Bank.

Directions

1. To make the body, measure and cut a 5-by-9-inch rectangle from white construction paper. Spread glue on it and wrap it around the juice can. Trace the lid pattern (FIG. 2-2) onto posterboard and cut it out. Cut a slit in it for money. Glue it on the top of the can. Turn the can over for a while to hold the lid until the glue dries.

2. Use the patterns in FIG. 2-2 to trace and cut out two black ears, two black paws, a black tail, a black nose, two large black eyes, two brown eyes, plus two black paper-punch eyeballs. Glue these on the body. Draw a mouth with a black marker.

3. Make a sign with white paper 3 by 4 inches. Fold the sign in half, and write a message on one side. Glue it onto the popsicle stick. Glue the stick under one paw as if the Giant Panda were holding it.

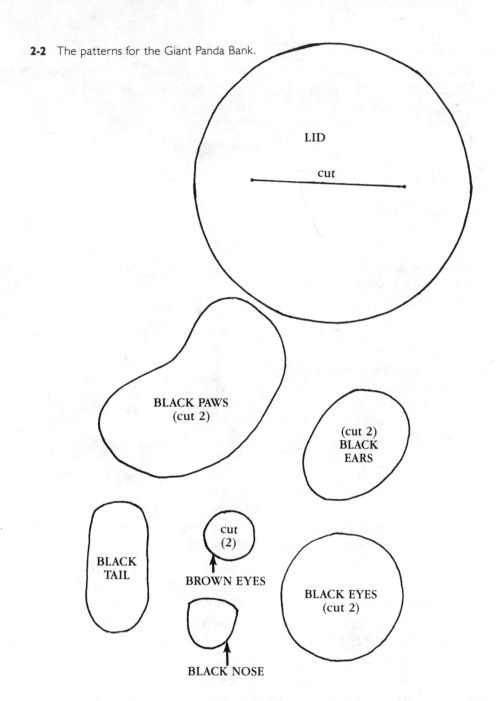

LID

cut

BLACK PAWS
(cut 2)

(cut 2)
BLACK
EARS

BLACK
TAIL

cut
(2)

BROWN EYES

BLACK EYES
(cut 2)

BLACK NOSE

woolie-pullie

Use a paper punch to make circles for eyes, eyeballs, noses, and tongues.

TEXAS LONGHORN BANK

Cattle with very long horns were raised by cowboys in the southwestern United States during the 1800s. Today's cattle have shorter—and safer—horns. This Texas Longhorn Bank will hold your moo-ney!

Materials List

- 12-ounce juice can
- Brown, yellow, white, and black construction paper
- Posterboard
- Ruler
- Scissors
- Black marker
- Elmer's Glue-All
- Paper punch
- Popsicle stick

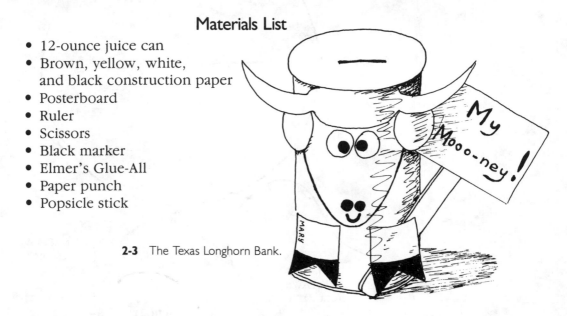

2-3 The Texas Longhorn Bank.

Directions

1. To make the body, measure and cut a 5-by-9-inch rectangle from brown construction paper. Spread glue on it and wrap it around the juice can. Trace the lid pattern (FIG. 2-4) onto posterboard. Cut it out. Cut a slit in it for money. Glue it on the top of the can. Turn the can upside down for a while to hold the lid on until the glue dries.

2. Use the rest of the patterns in FIG. 2-4 to trace and cut out the yellow horns, two brown ears, two brown feet, and two white eyes. Use a paper punch to make two black eyeballs and black nostrils.

3. Glue the horns at the top of the body. Use a black marker to draw the head in a long ∪ shape from one horn to the other. Glue on the ears, eyes, and paper-punch eyeballs and nostrils. Draw a mouth.

4. Color the tips of the feet black. Make a sign from white paper 3 by 4 inches. Fold the paper in half, and write a message on one side. Glue it onto the popsicle stick. Glue the feet on the front of the body. Glue one foot over the stick as if the Texas Longhorn were holding it.

5. Cut out a brown tail 4 by 1/4 inches. Fringe one end and glue it to the back of the bank.

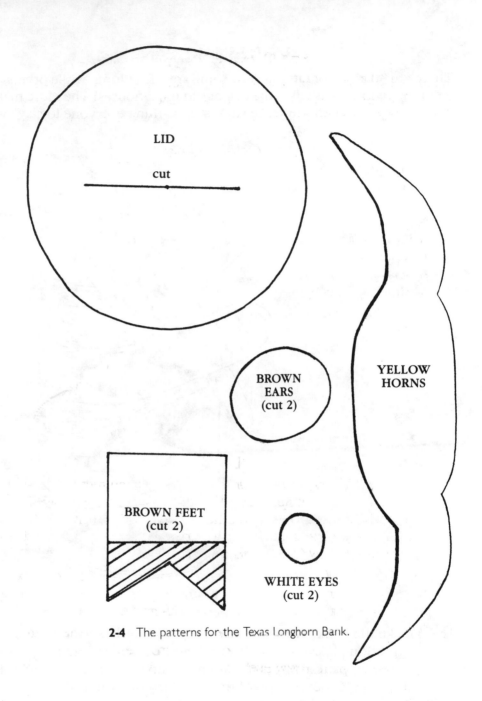

2-4 The patterns for the Texas Longhorn Bank.

RATTLESNAKE BANK

There are 30 kinds of rattlesnakes. Some are 1 foot long, while others are 8 feet long, which is as tall as the ceilings in most houses! The rattle makes a buzzing sound when the snake shakes it, warning everyone to stay away!

Materials List

- 12-ounce juice can
- Green and white construction paper
- Black marker
- Posterboard
- Ruler
- Scissors
- Elmer's Glue-All
- Popsicle stick

2-5 The Rattlesnake Bank.

Directions

1. To make the bank, measure and cut a 5-by-9-inch rectangle from white construction paper. Spread glue on it and wrap it around the juice can. Trace the lid pattern (FIG. 2-6) onto posterboard. Cut it out. Cut a slit in it for money. Glue it on top of the can. Turn the can upside down for a while to hold the lid on until the glue dries.

2. Measure and cut two green strips 1 by 12 inches. Use the patterns in FIG. 2-6 to trace the head on one strip and the rattle on the other strip. Cut out the head and rattle, and glue the strips together to make a long snake. Decorate it with the black marker.

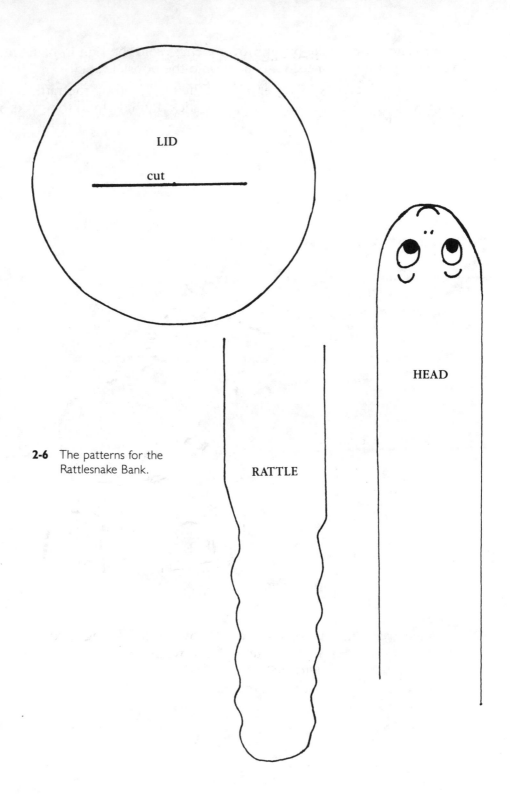

LID

cut

HEAD

RATTLE

2-6 The patterns for the Rattlesnake Bank.

3. Make a sign from white paper 3 by 4 inches. Fold the sign in half, and write a message on one side. Glue it onto the popsicle stick.

4. Put glue on the snake. Wrap it around the bank, letting the rattle and head stick out. Put glue on the popsicle stick. Put it behind the snake's head so it looks like the snake is holding it.

AFRICAN LION BANK

The lion is called "King of the Beasts" because the male lion has a majestic mane. He can grow to be 10 feet long and can weigh 500 pounds! Although the female lion is smaller and has no mane, she usually catches the food, and then brings it to her mate!

Materials List

- 12-ounce juice can
- Yellow, orange, black, and white construction paper
- Coffee filter
- Black and orange markers
- Posterboard
- Ruler
- Scissors
- Elmer's Glue-All
- Paper punch
- Popsicle stick

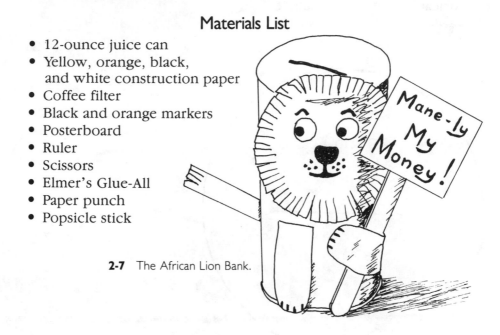

2-7 The African Lion Bank.

Directions

1. To make the body, measure and cut a 5-by-9-inch rectangle from yellow construction paper. Spread glue on it—don't get any on your clothes!—and wrap it around the juice can. Trace the lid pattern (FIG. 2-8) onto posterboard. Cut it out. Cut a slit in it for money. Glue it on the top of the can. Turn the can upside down for a while to hold the lid on until the glue dries.

2. Use the patterns in FIG. 2-8 to trace and cut out orange paws, white eyes, and a black nose. Make black paper-punch eyeballs. Draw an orange tail 4 by 1/2 inches. Cut it out and fringe one end.

3. To make the mane, fold the coffee filter in half three times. It will be shaped like a slice of pizza. Use the ruler to measure two inches from the tip of the "pizza" outward. Cut at the 2-inch mark and save the center piece. Open it and color it orange with a marker. Cut 1-inch slits all around the edge to fringe it. Glue the mane onto the front of the body.

4. Glue on eyes, black paper-punch eyeballs, nose, and tail. Use a black marker to draw a mouth and dots next to the mouth.

5. Make a sign from yellow paper 3 by 4 inches. Fold the sign in half, and write a message on one side. Glue it onto the popsicle stick. Glue the paws on the front of the body. Glue one paw over the stick as if the African Lion were holding it.

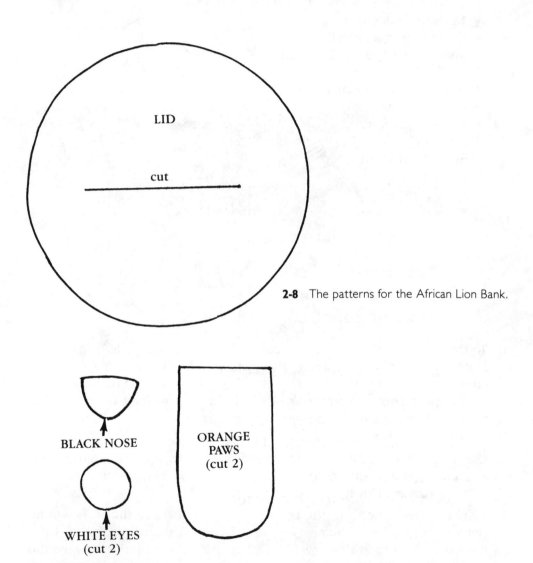

LID

cut

2-8 The patterns for the African Lion Bank.

BLACK NOSE

ORANGE
PAWS
(cut 2)

WHITE EYES
(cut 2)

3

Messy Materials

Use an old shirt
To cover up your clothes.
Lay newspaper on the table top;
You'll need a lot of those!

Get some flour and water
To make papier-mâché.
Also save old coffee grounds
To mix up Marbleized Clay.

Please just remember,
Don't make too big a mess.
I think you want your mom to say,
"More! Make more!"
Not, "LESS!!"

PAPIER-MÂCHÉ MASK

With flour, water, newspaper, and a balloon you can make a terrific mask!

Materials List

- Newspaper to cover work surface
- Newspaper torn into 1-inch strips
- Large bowl
- Wire whisk
- 9-inch balloon
- Flour
- Water
- Tempera paint
- Large and small watercolor brushes
- Scissors
- String

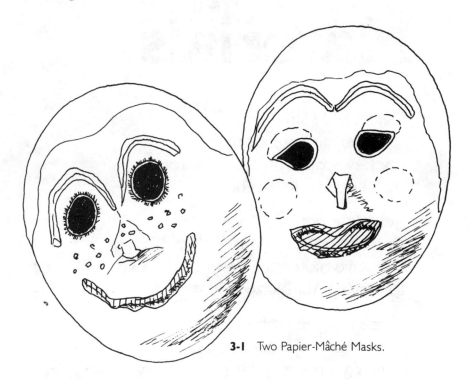

3-1 Two Papier-Mâché Masks.

Directions

1. Cover your work surface with newspaper. Wear an old shirt to cover up your clothes! Blow up the balloon until it is the same size as your head. Tie the end.

2. Make paste by mixing 1$^{1}/_{2}$ cups flour with 1 cup water in the bowl. Use the wire whisk to make the paste smooth.

3. Tear the newspaper strips into pieces 3 inches long. Dip a strip into the paste. Pull the strip between your fingers to remove extra paste. Smooth the strip onto the balloon. Add strips and paste until *half* of the balloon is covered. Do not cover the whole balloon. Only half is needed for your mask.

4. Cover your mask with a second layer of strips, then cover it again with a third layer.

5. To make a nose, crumple a piece of dry newspaper and hold it on the mask. Cover it with paste strips. To make eyebrows, twist pieces of newspaper and hold them on the mask where you want the eyes to be. Cover them with paste strips. Add lips the same way.

6. Now add a top layer of dry newspaper strips. Make sure the surface is smooth. Put your mask aside to dry for about a week. Turn it over every day so that it dries evenly and doesn't get moldy!

7. When the mask has dried *completely*, pop the balloon and throw it away. Trim the edges of the mask with scissors. Ask an adult to cut out the eyes and mouth for you.

8. Paint the entire mask the color of your face. Let the paint dry. Then paint on the mouth, eyes, and anything else you wish. Let the paint dry again. Punch holes in the sides of the mask; thread string through the holes and tie the mask around your head to wear it. Don't tie it too tight!

woolie-pullie

For easy papier-mâché cleanup, use a washcloth and dish detergent to rub paste off hands while holding them under running water. Put dish detergent in an empty soft-soap dispenser for a fast squirt!

MARBLEIZED CLAY ON WOOD

The wood is stained with coffee. Grounds go into the clay. The clay looks just like marble. Don't give the secret away!

Materials List

- Large bowl
- 1 cup flour
- 1/4 cup salt
- 6 tablespoons water
- 1 tablespoon coffee grounds (Used grounds are OK.)
- Baking sheet covered with aluminum foil
- Piece of wood (I used a piece 6 by 8 by 3/4 inches.)
- Sandpaper
- Strong cold coffee
- Newspaper
- Varnish or spray shellac
- Elmer's Glue-All

3-2 Marbleized Clay on Wood.

Directions

1. Put the flour, salt, water, and coffee grounds in a bowl. Mix it to make clay. Add more flour if it is sticky. Mold the clay into any shape you like. You can make your initials or your name, or a cross or a ram's horn.

2. Lay the clay shapes on the baking sheet. Ask an adult to help you bake them at 350 °F for 20 minutes. Turn the clay over. If it is still soft it can be baked for a few more minutes. Do not let it get brown. Leave it in a turned-off oven to dry out.

3. Sand the wood until it is smooth. Dip it in cold coffee to stain it. Let it dry completely.

4. Cover your work space with newspaper. Glue the marbleized clay shapes on the wood. Ask an adult to help you make it shiny with varnish or spray shellac.

___woolie-pullie___

Wood crafts take longer to make than paper crafts. The wood must dry after being stained and glued. After you begin a wood craft, start another project while the wood dries.

CLAY DIORAMA ON WOOD

Our clay is flour-salt dough. It's fun to make, easy to use, and costs very little. This diorama has a volcano that erupts.

Materials List

- 4 cups flour
- 1 cup salt
- 1 1/2 cups water
- Large bowl
- Red, green, blue, and yellow liquid food dye
- Board (I used a wood square 9 by 9 by 1/2 inches.)
- Several miniature dinosaurs, 2 inches long. (Look in a party supply store.)
- 1 teaspoon baking soda
- 1 teaspoon vinegar
- Small rocks, seashells, twigs (optional)

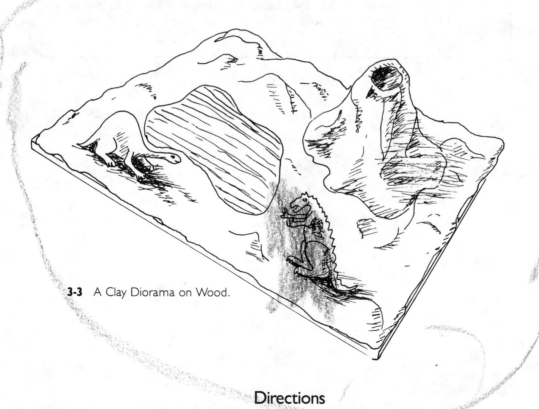

3-3 A Clay Diorama on Wood.

Directions

1. Measure the flour, salt, and water into the bowl. Mix it into a dough. Divide the dough into pieces. Make a hole in one piece and squirt in

green food color. Divide the remaining dough into two pieces. Dye one piece blue. Follow the directions on the box of food colors to dye the last piece brown. Squeeze the dough to spread the color.

2. Spread the green clay all over the top of the board. Add a blue clay lake. Shape the brown clay into a volcano. Make a hole in the top of the volcano with your finger.

3. Put your dinosaurs on the diorama. You can add rocks, twigs, and seashells.

4. Let the diorama dry for a week. To make the volcano erupt, put one teaspoon of baking soda in the top. Then add one teaspoon of vinegar. Try this in a cup before you put it in your volcano.

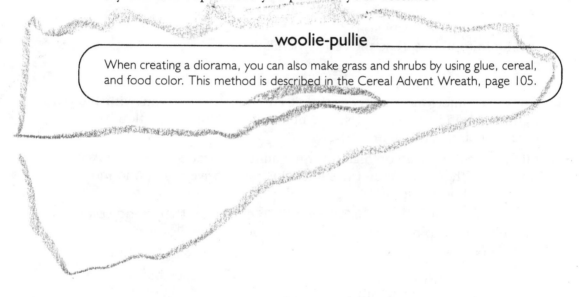

woolie-pullie

When creating a diorama, you can also make grass and shrubs by using glue, cereal, and food color. This method is described in the Cereal Advent Wreath, page 105.

THREE-MINUTE PLAY DOUGH

Homemade play dough is fun because you can dye it any color you wish. Follow the directions on the back of the food dye box to make orange, purple, or even brown. This dough stays soft.

Materials List

- Large bowl for the microwave
- Electric mixer
- 1 cup water
- 1 cup flour
- 1/2 cup salt
- 2 teaspoons cream of tartar
- 1 tablespoon vegtable oil
- Liquid food dye (Use the color you like best.)

Directions

1. These are microwave directions. Ask an adult to help you with the microwave and the mixer. Use the mixer to mix the water, flour, salt, cream of tartar, and oil in the bowl.

2. Microwave the dough on high for three minutes. Beat it with the mixer until smooth. If the dough is still sticky, microwave it for one more minute and beat it again.

3. Divide the dough into balls. Poke a hole in each ball. Drop food color in the hole and pinch it shut. Squeeze the dough to color it.

4. Store the play dough in the refrigerator in a plastic bag to keep it fresh.

NOTE: If you make this recipe with baby oil instead of vegetable oil, it will stay fresh at room temperature. It can also be cooked on top of the stove. Put the ingredients in a pot. Cook the mixture over high heat, stirring constantly until a stiff ball forms.

4

Coffee Filter Crafts

Don't bother to cut a circle;
A filter comes ready-made.
Take lots of snips with scissors
To make a starched snowflake.

A flower in bloom
And a fragrant sachet
Are some of the crafts
You can make today!

COFFEE FILTER SNOWFLAKES

Coffee filters give us a perfect circle. They are tough, yet they are easy to cut. These snowflakes are starched for stiffness.

Materials List

- 2 coffee filters
- Scissors
- Small bowl or Styrofoam tray
- Liquid starch (Look among the laundry soaps in the grocery store.)
- Wax paper
- Glitter
- Sewing needle
- White thread

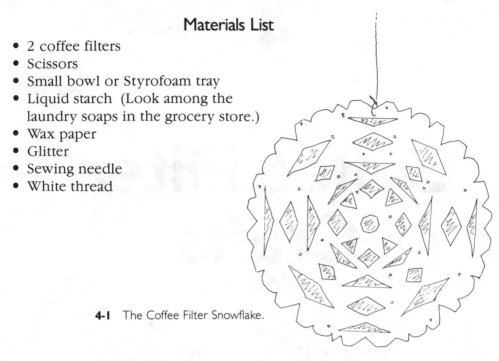

4-1 The Coffee Filter Snowflake.

Directions

1. Fold each coffee filter in half three times so it looks like a small piece of pie (FIG. 4-2).

2. On one coffee filter cut out half-circles from both sides and from the edge. Cut off the tip. On the other coffee filter cut out small triangles from both sides and the edge. Fold each one in half a fourth time and cut two or three half-circles or triangles.

3. Pour 2 tablespoons liquid starch into a small bowl or Styrofoam tray. Lay one folded snowflake in the starch. Pick up the snowflake and press it with your fingers until all the dry, white spots are soaked with starch.

4. Open the snowflake. Spread it on wax paper. Sprinkle with glitter. Let it dry completely. Repeat with the other snowflake.

5. Use a needle and white thread to sew a loop in the edge of the dry snowflake. Don't prick yourself! Hang the snowflake from the ceiling with straight pins, or tie the thread to a paper clip. Insert the paper clip under the metal edge of a false ceiling in the classroom.

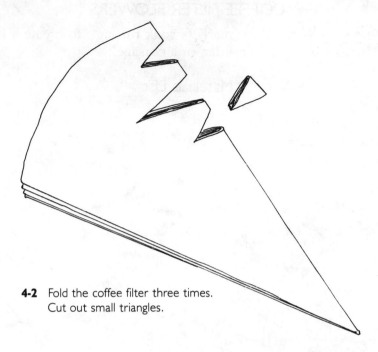

4-2 Fold the coffee filter three times.
Cut out small triangles.

COFFEE FILTER FLOWERS

Coffee filters let water-based markers soak through to create a beautiful design. Use as a bouquet, a border, or a corsage!

Materials List

- Coffee filter
- Water in a small bowl
- Water-base markers
- Pipe cleaner

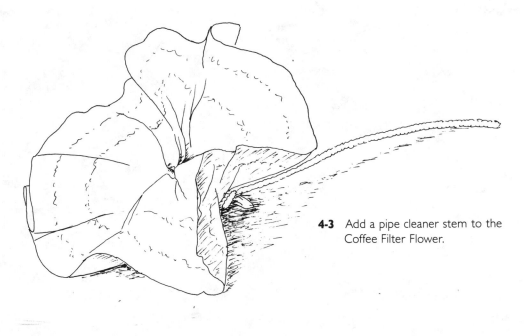

4-3 Add a pipe cleaner stem to the Coffee Filter Flower.

Directions

1. Fold the coffee filter in half three times so it looks like a small piece of pie.
2. Dip it in water (FIG. 4-4). Strip off the extra water with your fingers.
3. Color the wet, folded coffee filter with markers. You can make stripes, dots, and zigzags. Turn the filter over. Repeat the design that you just colored. This will help the design soak all the way through the filter.
4. Open the filter-flower and let it dry completely.
5. To make a flower, put your finger in the middle of the filter. Pinch the filter around the tip of your finger. Twist the middle. Wrap a pipe cleaner stem around the twisted middle.

4-4 Fold the coffee filter three times. Dip it in water.

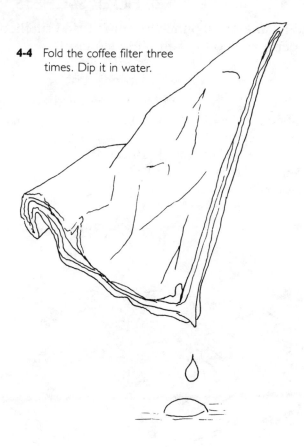

COFFEE FILTER SACHETS

A Coffee Filter Flower, punched, stuffed, and stitched, turns into a sachet when a perfumed cotton ball is hidden inside.

Materials List

- Cotton ball dipped in cologne or aftershave
- Coffee Filter Flower (Page 42.)
- Paper punch
- Synthetic stuffing or 15 cotton balls
- 15-inch narrow, crimped ribbon
- Scissors

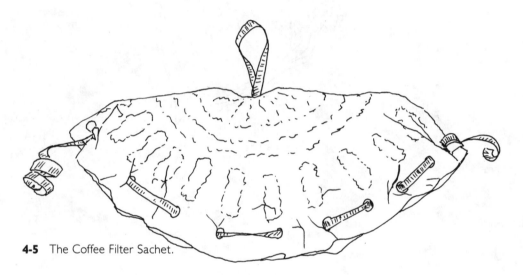

4-5 The Coffee Filter Sachet.

Directions

1. After the Coffee Filter Flower has completely dried, fold it in half. Use the paper punch to make holes through both layers around the edges (FIG. 4-6).

2. Tie one end of the ribbon through the holes at one side, then lace the ribbon half-way around the sachet (FIG. 4-6).

3. Fill the sachet with stuffing or cotton balls. Put the perfumed cotton ball inside the stuffing.

4. Lace the ribbon the rest of the way around. Tie it at the end. Curl the ribbon ends with the scissors. Have an adult show you how.

4-6 Punch holes around the edges. Lace with ribbon.

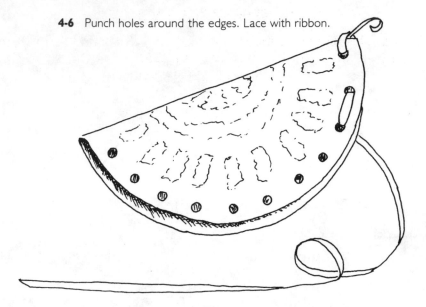

5. Cut a very small hole in the top of the sachet. Dip one end of a 5-inch ribbon in Elmer's Glue-All. Stick it in the hole and pinch the hole shut. Let this dry. The sachet can be hung in the closet or placed in a drawer to make clothes smell nice.

5

Tissue Paper Art

Did you ever get
Tissue paper wet?
It runs and drips its colors.

Use it wet to make
Patterns so great,
Or use it dry for tissue flowers.

RIP-N-DRIP CLOUD PAINTING

For this craft, use tissue paper whose color runs or bleeds when you get it wet. Your finished picture can be used as a background for black paper birds, boats, or geometric shapes. Laminate it to make a place mat.

Materials List

- 6 colors of tissue paper, such as red, orange, purple, blue, yellow, and green
- Hair spray bottle filled with water
- White construction paper
- Black construction paper (optional)
- Scissors (optional)
- Elmer's Glue-All (optional)

5-1 Rip-N-Drip Cloud Painting.

Directions

1. Cut the tissue paper into 6-inch squares. Use two squares of each color. Tear each square into four or more pieces. Lay the pieces all over the sheet of white construction paper. Let some pieces overlap (FIG. 5-2).

5-2 Lay torn tissue on white paper. Let some pieces overlap.

2. Use the spray bottle to squirt a thin layer of water over the whole picture. Pat the tissues with your fingers to press them onto the white paper. Now let the picture dry completely.

3. Lift off the dry tissues. Divide the tissues into a stack of light colors (red, orange, yellow) and a stack of dark colors (purple, blue, green). Wad each stack into a ball and wet it with the spray bottle.

4. Use the balls of wet tissue to stipple (dot up and down) color onto white areas of your cloud painting.

5. You can use black construction paper to add birds sailing across the clouds, or to make boats at sunset. You can add black geometric shapes or glue and glitter. Laminate your Rip-N-Drip Cloud Painting to make a place mat. No one will ever guess how you painted it!

WATER FLOWERS

For this craft, choose tissue paper whose color runs or bleeds when you get it wet. Use the Water Flowers to border a poem, or cut and glue them to create a unique flower picture.

Materials List

- 6 colors of tissue paper, such as red, orange, purple, blue, yellow, and green.
- Hair spray bottle filled with water
- Scissors
- Elmer's Glue-All
- White construction paper or posterboard

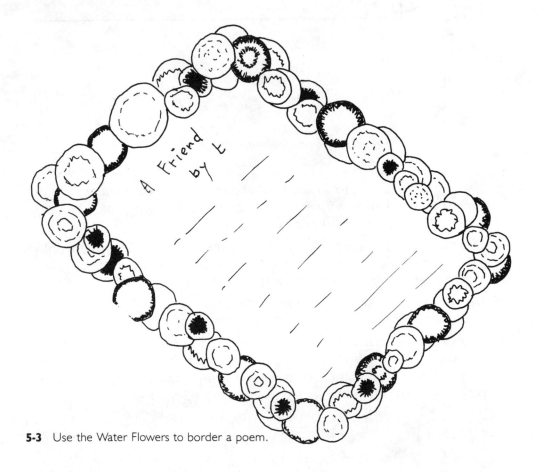

5-3 Use the Water Flowers to border a poem.

Directions

1. Cut the tissue paper into 6-inch squares. Use one square of each color. Lay the squares on top of each other to make a stack.

2. Hold the spray bottle close to the stack of tissues. Squirt water to make a small circle on the tissues. Repeat this to make as many circles as you can, but do not let the circles touch each other. The circles must stay apart, like pancakes frying in a skillet (FIG. 5-4).

5-4 Drip circles of water on the stacked tissue squares.

3. Turn the stack over. Make more circles if there is dry space. Press on the stack with your fingers. Now let it dry completely.

4. Separate the sheets of tissue. The water has made multi-colored circles called Water Flowers. Cut these out.

5. Write a poem on white construction paper or posterboard. Dot glue around the edges of the paper. Glue the flowers all around the edges.

6. Make a flower picture from the cut-out Water Flowers.

Here is a poem you can use with your Water Flowers.

A Friend
by Elizabeth Dondiego

You are a shoulder to cry on,
A girl to rely on,
A kind voice that speaks up in the dark.
A pal and a buddy,
A gal to help study,
Someone braver than Joan of Arc.
But most of all . . .
You're a friend.
Together we change and we bend.
We seek different goals,
And may grow apart,
But we'll always be friends in the heart.

SUNBEAM GLISTENER

The Sunbeam Glistener sticks to a window, but peels off easily. It looks beautiful when the sun shines through it.

Materials List

- Styrofoam meat tray
- Plastic wrap
- Elmer's Glue-All
- Tissue paper scraps of all colors

5-5 The Sunbeam Glistener on a window pane.

Directions

1. Line the Styrofoam tray with plastic wrap. Squirt on glue in heavy swirls. Lay tissue paper scraps on the glue. Use lots of different colors.

Overlap the scraps when you lay them in the glue, but try to keep them in a single layer.

2. Let this dry for three days, or until all the whiteness of wet glue has disappeared.

3. Peel off the plastic wrap. Lay a pattern from FIG. 5-6 on the Sunbeam Glistener and cut it into a shape with scissors.

4. Press the shiny side against a glass window pane.

5-6 A pattern for the Sunbeam Glistener.

GLADIOLUS TISSUE FLOWERS

This beautiful flower doesn't look exactly like a real gladiolus, but it's close enough. Make it any color you wish out of bright tissue paper.

Materials List

- Facial tissue
- Green tissue paper, plus any other color you wish
- Posterboard
- Pencil
- Scissors
- 11-inch pipe cleaner
- Elmer's Glue-All

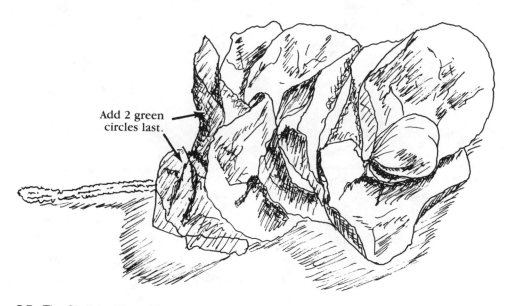

Add 2 green circles last.

5-7 The Gladiolus Tissue Flower.

Directions

1. Use the pattern in FIG. 5-8 to cut out two green tissue paper circles. Use the same pattern to cut out 10 tissue paper circles in a bright color of your choice. The green circles go on last.

2. Crumple the facial tissue into a ball. Cover it with a tissue paper circle. Hold it on the end of the pipe cleaner and twist the tissue paper around the pipe cleaner to keep it in place (FIG. 5-9). This is the top of the flower.

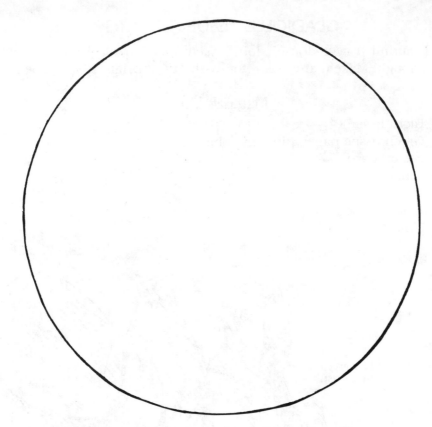

5-8 The pattern for the Gladiolus and Poppy Tissue Flowers.

3. Bend up three inches of pipe cleaner at the bottom (FIG. 5-9). This will make the stem stronger.

4. Wad up the nine tissue paper circles into a ball. (Save the two green ones.) Squeeze them. Open them. Squeeze them into a ball again. Open them again. Flatten them out with your fingers.

5. Apply glue to the pipe cleaner just below the ball at the top. Wrap the edge of one circle around the pipe cleaner. Most of the circle will stick out to look like a flower petal (FIG. 5-9). Add each circle the same way, one at a time. Move down the pipe cleaner a little with each circle as you glue it on. The two green circles will go last and will wrap around the tip of the folded pipe cleaner to hold it in place (FIG. 5-7). These are leaves.

6. Curl the edge of each flower petal under by rolling it around a pencil.

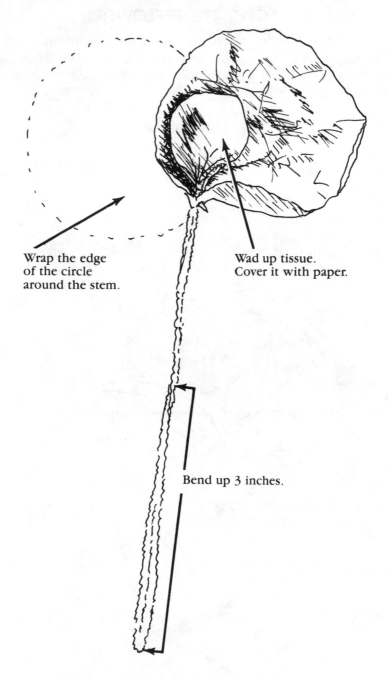

Wrap the edge
of the circle
around the stem.

Wad up tissue.
Cover it with paper.

Bend up 3 inches.

5-9 How to make a Gladiolus Tissue Flower.

POPPY TISSUE FLOWERS

Real poppies have bright, papery petals that look beautiful in a flower garden. The poppy put Dorothy to sleep in the movie, *The Wizard of Oz*. Its tiny seeds, which do not make us sleepy, are used to make delicious breads, cakes, and cookies.

Materials List

- Facial tissue
- Tissue paper of yellow, green, and another bright color
- Posterboard
- Pencil
- Scissors
- 11-inch pipe cleaner
- Elmer's Glue-All

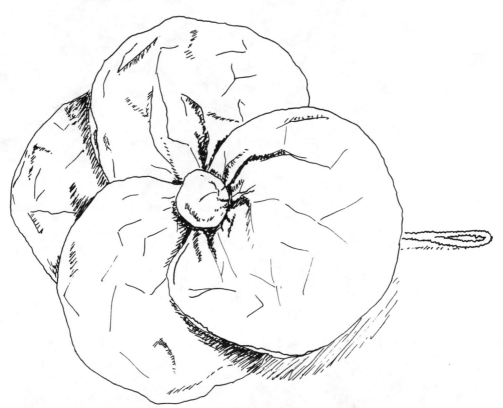

5-10 The Poppy Tissue Flower.

Directions

1. Use the pattern in FIG. 5-8 to cut out one yellow tissue paper circle, two green circles, and four circles of another bright color.

2. Wad the facial tissue into a ball. Cover it with the yellow circle. Bend the pipe cleaner in half. Hold the ball on the end of the pipe cleaner and twist the tissue around the pipe cleaner to keep it in place (FIG. 5-11). This is the center of the poppy.

3. Wad the four tissue paper circles into a ball. (Save the green ones.) Squeeze them. Open them. Squeeze them into a ball again. Flatten them out with your fingers.

4. Apply glue to the pipe cleaner just below the ball at the top. Wrap the edge of one circle around the pipe cleaner. Most of the circle will stick out to look like a flower petal (FIG. 5-11). Add each circle the same way, one at a time around the center. Glue on the two green circles below the flower petals; these are the leaves.

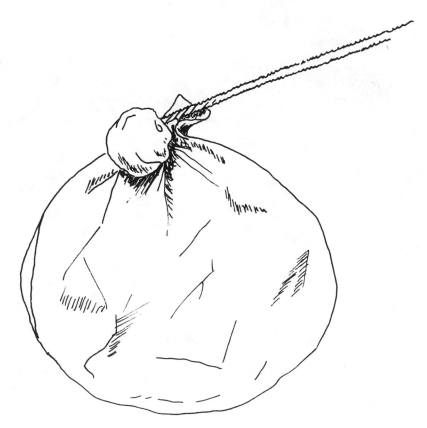

5-11 Apply glue below the ball on top. Wrap the edge of the circle around the stem.

6

Crafts from Lids

Instead of taking lids off,
And throwing them away,
Save them for another day.

Dot a milk lid
With colored glue!
Make a frame
For a picture of you!

MILK LIDS AND COLORED GLUE

Make your own colored glue by adding food colors to Elmer's Glue-All. A milk lid is a surprising canvas!

Materials List

- Milk lid, complete with outer safety circle
- Posterboard
- Pencil
- Scissors
- Cotton ball
- 3-inch square of white cloth (Use an old handkerchief, sheet, or shirt.)
- 1½-inch strip magnet. (Buy strip magnets in a craft store.)
- Cellophane tape
- Elmer's Glue-All
- Wax paper
- Red, green, blue, and yellow liquid food dye
- 4 round toothpicks, one for each color

6-1 A Milk Lid with Colored Glue.

Directions

1. Use the milk lid as a pattern to draw a circle on the posterboard. Cut out the circle and set it aside.

2. Put the cotton ball on top of the milk lid. Drape the cloth over it. Press the outer safety circle over the cloth until it fits around the milk lid. It will hold the cloth in place. Cut off the extra cloth.

3. Apply glue around the bottom rim of the milk lid. Press on the posterboard circle. Add the strip magnet. Use cellophane tape to hold the circle in place until it dries.

4. On a sheet of wax paper squirt four pools of glue, ½ teaspoon each. Add one drop of food color to each pool to make red glue, yellow glue, green glue, and blue glue. Stir each color with its own toothpick.

5. Use the toothpicks to drop dots of color on the cloth-covered milk lid. Do not let the dots touch or they will run together and your milk lid will turn black! Add more dots in an hour, using the same glue pools. The glue will thicken as it sits, and you can add new dots of color to your milk lid each hour or so.

6. When the lid is completely dry, use it to hold notes on anything metal.

woolie-pullie

Empty cereal boxes can be used as posterboard for some crafts. Use them as posterboard circles in this chapter. Use them to make sturdy pattern pieces, too.

MAGNETIC PICTURE FRAME

A shiny canning lid makes a perfect picture frame. Add a strip magnet to display a photo on your refrigerator or locker door.

Materials List

- Band and lid from regular Ball Mason caps (Look in the canning/freezing section of the grocery store.)
- Posterboard
- Pencil
- Scissors
- Favorite photograph
- Facial tissue
- Elmer's Glue-All
- 3-inch strip magnet (Buy strip magnet in a craft store.)

6-2 The Magnetic Picture Frame.

Directions

1. Use the band and the lid as patterns to draw two circles on the posterboard. Cut out the circles.

2. Use the lid as a pattern to cut the photograph: Place the lid on the photograph; trace around it; cut it out. Put the photo in the band.

3. Place the smaller posterboard circle on the back of the photo. Lightly wad up the facial tissue. Put it on the posterboard circle. The tissue will help hold the photo in place without adding weight. Do not use the metal lid; it is only a pattern for this craft.

4. The picture frame should be upside down. Apply glue to the edge of the band. Place the larger posterboard circle on it. Stick the 3-inch strip magnet on the posterboard. Let this dry upside down with a heavy book on top to keep it flat.

CANNING LID PINCUSHION

Even if a person doesn't sew, a pincushion is a handy place to stick pins from the dry cleaner, or to save a needle to replace a button.

Materials List

- Band and lid from regular Ball Mason caps (Look in the canning/freezing section of the grocery store.)
- Posterboard
- Pencil
- Scissors
- 4$^1/2$-inch square of cloth
- Synthetic stuffing (fiber-fill)
- Elmer's Glue-All
- Ribbon 10 by $^1/2$ inches

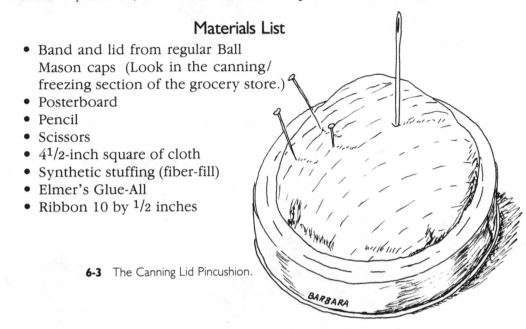

6-3 The Canning Lid Pincushion.

Directions

1. Use the band as a pattern to draw a circle on the posterboard. Cut out the circle and set it aside.

2. Turn the band upside down. Spread the cloth over it. Put a small handful of stuffing on the cloth. Press the lid on the stuffing until it snaps into the band.

3. Trim the extra corners of the cloth. Fold the rest of the cloth onto the lid.

4. Apply Glue-All around the inside edge of the band. Lay the posterboard circle on the band. Press the circle completely into the band.

5. Put glue around the outside edges of the band. Wrap the ribbon around the band. Set your pincushion aside to dry.

7

Empty Egg Crafts

Blow and rinse and dry the egg;
A craft you then can make.
The outside becomes a Sugar Egg;
The inside becomes pancakes!

HOW TO BLOW OUT AN EGG

The secret to blowing out an egg is to break the yolk, then blow!

Materials List

- Raw egg
- Darning needle or corsage pin
- Bowl
- Water to rinse the shell

Directions

1. Use a darning needle or corsage pin to poke a hole in one end of the egg. Do not use a knife. It will cut you!

2. Carefully take away bits of shell to widen the hole to about $1/8$ inch. Stick the pin into the egg and stir the raw egg inside the shell to break the yellow yolk.

3. Use the pin to make another hole in the other end of the egg. Put this end tightly against your mouth and blow into the egg, while you hold it over the bowl. The insides will blow out.

4. Rinse the inside of the shell by filling it with water. Shake out the water. Let the shell dry. Use it to make an Easter Egg Plant.

EASTER EGG PLANT

Easter eggs have been a sign of renewed life for hundreds of years. Hang decorated eggs on a tree branch to create your own Easter Egg Plant!

Materials List

- Plaster of paris. (Buy this in a hardware store.)
- 10-ounce plastic beverage cup
- Tree branch 12 to 15 inches high
- Water
- 3 blown-out eggs
- Narrow ribbon
- Markers
- Sequins or glitter
- Tissue wrapping paper

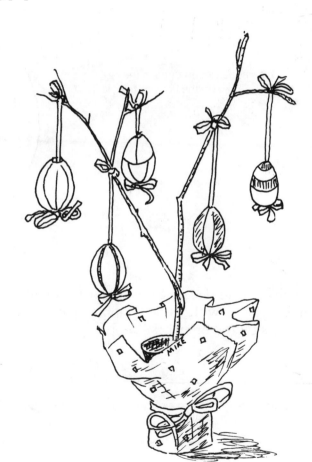

7-1 The Easter Egg Plant.

Directions

1. Put plaster of paris in the plastic beverage cup until the cup is half full. Stir in water until the plaster is as thick as cake batter. Put the end of the tree branch in the middle of the cup. Prop it against something sturdy until the plaster becomes firm. This takes about 20 minutes. Meanwhile, get the eggs ready to hang.

2. Look on page 68 to learn how to blow out an egg. Insert a narrow ribbon through one end of the egg and pull it out the other end. Tie three big, loose knots in one end of the ribbon to hold the egg, or tie a bow on one end of the ribbon (FIG. 7-2). The bow will look nice and will keep the egg from sliding off the ribbon.

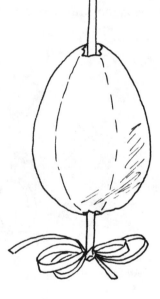

7-2 Put a ribbon through the egg. Tie a bow on the bottom to hold it.

3. Use markers to decorate the eggs. Glue on glitter or sequins. Cover the cup of plaster with tissue wrapping paper. Tie a ribbon around it. Tie the eggs on the branches.

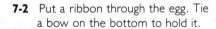

woolie-pullie

Turn the Easter Plant into a seasonal tree by replacing the eggs with tiny snowflakes, fall leaves, or paper flowers.

SUGAR EGG

Cover an egg with sugar frosting. Put a small plastic figure or photograph of a friend inside to create a magical scene!

Materials List

- Large egg
- Egg white from one large egg (Save the yolk for cooking.)
- 1 3/4 cups powdered sugar
- Liquid food dye
- Small plastic figure from a craft store, or a photograph
- Milk lid
- Glitter
- Glue
- Wax paper
- Bowl
- Spoon

7-3 Make a hole in the side of an egg. Then make the Sugar Egg.

Directions

1. Use a needle to open the side of the egg. Then break off tiny pieces of eggshell with your fingers until there is an oval opening in the egg (FIG. 7-3). Separate the egg white from the yolk. Ask an adult to help you. Put the egg white in the bowl. Rinse the empty eggshell with water. Let it dry.

2. To make the sugar frosting, add the powdered sugar to the egg white

and mix well. You can add food dye to part of the frosting if you want a multi-colored egg.

3. Put wax paper on your work surface. Hold the egg in your hand and spread frosting all over the outside with the back of the spoon. Set the frosted egg in the milk lid; the lid will be the base. Spoon a little frosting inside the egg, too.

4. Dip your finger into the frosting. Dab more frosting around the egg opening. You can use a different color for this if you wish. You can also drip strands of different-colored frosting from your finger onto the egg for a nice effect. Set the egg aside and let it dry for two days.

5. Dip the bottom of the small plastic figure (or the photograph) in glue and set it inside the egg. Spread a little glue inside the egg. Shake in glitter. It will stick to the glue, and you can shake the extra glitter out of the egg.

6. Use a butter knife to trim the extra frosting from the milk lid. Glue a ribbon around the milk lid base.

7. One egg white makes $1/2$ cup frosting which is enough to make six Sugar Eggs.

8

Mosaic Materials

Crush some eggshells;
Add some dye;
Make a design of mosaic!

Color some pasta;
Let it dry;
Glue a Festive Hot Plate!

EGGSHELLS UNDER THE SEA

Eggshells make perfect fish scales for sea creatures. Although the whale is a warm-blooded mammal instead of a fish, this whale looks perfect clad in "egg-scales."

Materials List

- Eggshells from at least 6 eggs
- 4 plastic sandwich bags with twist ties
- Red, green, blue, and yellow liquid food dye
- Paper towels
- Posterboard
- Scissors
- Pencil
- Elmer's Glue-All
- Construction paper

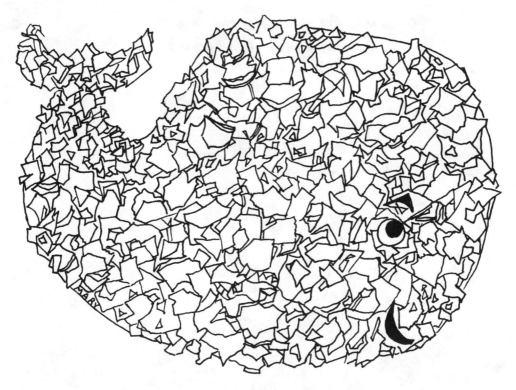

8-1 Eggshells Under the Sea.

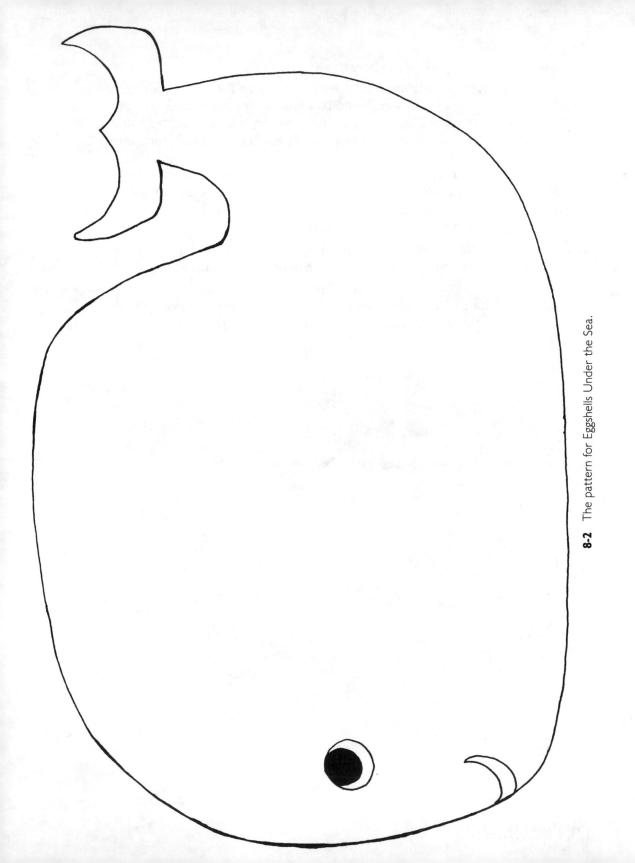

Directions

1. Divide the eggshells among four plastic bags. Drip food dye into each bag. Dye one bag of shells *red,* one bag *blue,* one *green,* and one *yellow.* Close each bag with a twist tie. Shake the bags to spread the color. Pour the colored shells onto paper towels to dry. Crunch them into small pieces after they dry.

2. Use the pattern in FIG. 8-2 to trace and cut out a posterboard whale. Spread glue on one-fourth of the whale, and pile on one color of shells. Spread glue on another part of the whale, and pile on a second color of shells. Continue adding glue and shells until the whale is covered.

3. Let the whale dry under a heavy book to keep it flat. Add a paper eye and a mouth by cutting them from construction paper and gluing them on.

4. Glue your whale to a larger picture, decorating a room or a poster with him, or put a thread through his top and hang him up.

FESTIVE HOT PLATE

This hot plate keeps hot dishes from touching the table. It is made of short pasta called *ditali*. You can also make the hot plate from beans of different colors.

Materials List

- Bag of *ditali* pasta
- 4 jars with lids
- Red, green, blue, and yellow liquid food dye
- Newspaper
- Posterboard
- Ruler
- Pencil
- Scissors
- Aluminum foil
- Elmer's Glue-All

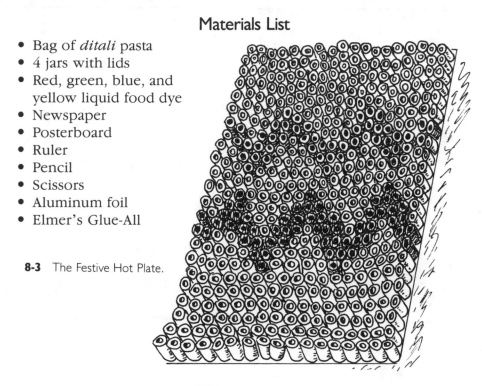

8-3 The Festive Hot Plate.

Directions

1. Divide the pasta among the four jars. Squirt one food color in each jar to make red pasta, yellow pasta, green pasta, and blue pasta. Add a spoonful of water to each jar to help spread the color. Put the lids on tightly. Shake the jars.

2. Drain the dye from the jars. Spread the colored ditali on newspaper to dry. Let it dry for one day.

3. Measure and cut out a 6-by-8-inch rectangle from posterboard. Squirt glue on it in a zigzag line. Use one color of the ditali at a time; stand each piece of pasta on end in the glue. Add more glue and use a second color of ditali. Keep adding glue and pasta until your rectangle is filled.

4. Place a piece of aluminum foil on the Festive Hot Plate. Put a book on it to keep it flat. Don't use a book that's too heavy or the pasta will crumble. Let your Hot Plate dry for one day.

woolie-pullie

Ditali is a short, straight macaroni. Sometimes it's called *Chili Macs*. If you can't find ditali in the grocery store, make the Festive Hot Plate with dry beans of different colors.

SAND PAINTING

Native Americans created beautiful pictures on the ground with colored sand as part of their religious ceremonies. You can make a design by using dry cereal such as Cream of Wheat, Cream of Rice, or grits. Your Sand Painting can decorate a square, a cross, or a ram's horn.

Materials List

- Posterboard
- Scissors
- Pen
- Ruler
- Wax paper
- Milk lid
- Elmer's Glue-All
- Small watercolor brush
- Dry grits or Cream of Wheat or Cream of Rice
- Red, green, blue, and yellow liquid food dye
- Plastic sandwich bags with twist ties

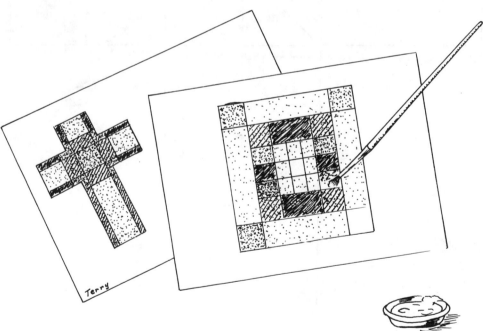

8-4 Sand Painting.

Directions

1. Cut a 6-inch square from posterboard, or use the patterns in FIGS. 8-5 and 8-6 to draw and cut out a cross or a ram's horn. Use the pen and ruler to draw large squares and rectangles on your shape.

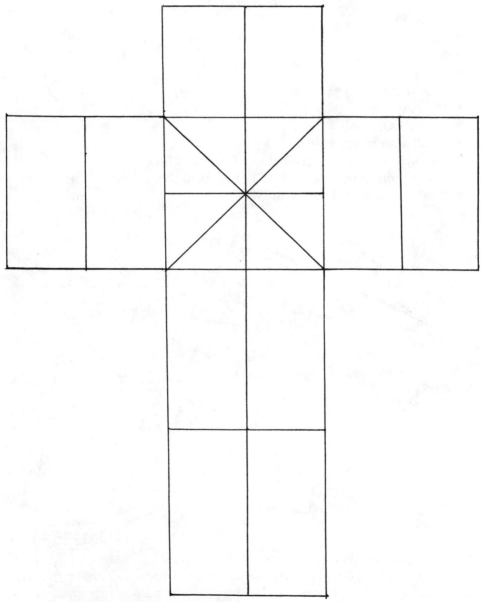

8-5 A Cross for Sand Painting.

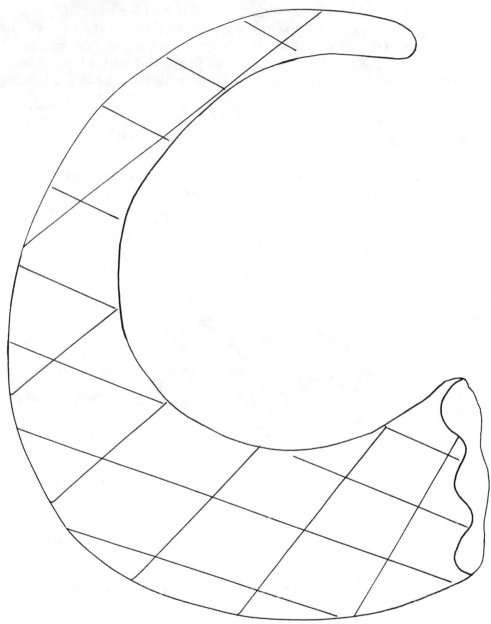

8-6 A Ram's Horn for Sand Painting.

2. Pour one tablespoon of dry cereal into a plastic sandwich bag. Add three drops of food dye. Close the bag with a twist tie. Shake the bag until the cereal is colored. Do the same thing with three more sandwich bags, adding a different color to each bag.

3. Put wax paper under your work. Squirt glue into the milk lid. Dip the brush into the glue, then paint the glue onto some of the squares on your shape (FIG. 8-4). Sprinkle one color of cereal onto the wet glue. Shake off the extra cereal onto the wax paper and return it to its bag. Continue painting a few squares at a time with glue, adding different colors each time.

4. When your shape is covered with colored cereal, lay it flat to dry. If it starts to curl up, put a piece of wax paper on it and put a heavy book on top until it dries.

5. Wash out your brush with soap and water. Glue your shape onto a piece of cardboard or construction paper to display it after it dries.

Using a little imagination, any child can transform ordinary household materials into a fire-breathing dragon.

Julia, Chris, and Jeff proudly display their colorful juice-can animals.

Step one for the papier-mâché mask. Jeff holds the bowl as Kathy adds water to the flour.

Step two for the papier-mâché mask. As Jeff watches, Kathy stirs the flour-and-water mixture.

Jeff and Kathy display the finished papier-mâché mask.

Samantha and Chris with the finished bi-plane.

Crafting can be fun! Julia, Chris, Lucas, Samantha, Kathy, and Jeff with fire-breathing dragon, dinosaurs, and juice-can animals.

9

Crafts from Empty Containers

Cover a shoebox
To make a hound.
Design a Baby Food Snow Dome.

Eat some butter;
Then make a clown.
It's fun to recycle at home!

HOW TO COVER A SHOEBOX

A shoebox is too good to throw away! It's made of sturdy paper, has a lid, and holds lots of things. Cover it with construction paper and turn it into anything you wish!

Materials List

- Shoebox
- Construction paper
- Ruler
- Scissors
- Elmer's Glue-All
- Cellophane tape

Directions

1. Shoeboxes come in different sizes. You can use a ruler to measure the sides and end of your box so you will know how to cut the construction paper, or you can press the paper against the box and cut on the crease marks. The following directions will use the ruler method.

2. Take the lid off the box. Use a ruler to measure one end of the lid. Cut two pieces of construction paper that are as wide as the end, but are two inches taller. Glue one paper on each end of the lid (FIG. 9-1).

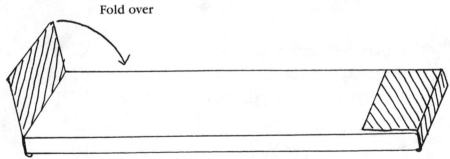

Fold over

9-1 Glue one paper on each end of the lid.

3. Measure the top of the lid. Cut out paper that is just as long as the top, but is three inches wider than the sides. Glue the paper on the lid, wrapping it down the sides and under the side edges (FIG. 9-2). Use tape inside the lid to hold the paper in place until the glue dries. Don't put tape on the outside of your box where it can be seen. Tape isn't very pretty.

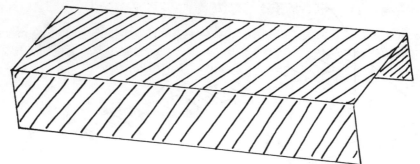

9-2 Glue the paper on the lid.

4. To cover the bottom of the box, use a ruler to measure one end. Cut two pieces of paper that are as tall as the end, but are two inches wider. Glue one paper on each end, wrapping it around both sides of the box (FIG. 9-3).

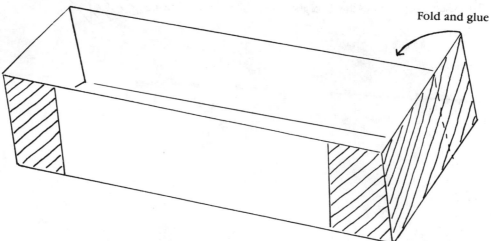

Fold and glue

9-3 Glue one paper on each end of the box.

5. Measure the sides of the box. Cut out two pieces of paper that are as wide as the sides, but are one inch taller. Glue one paper on each side, folding the taller part of the paper into the box (FIG. 9-4). Use your covered box to make the next craft, a Shoebox Hound.

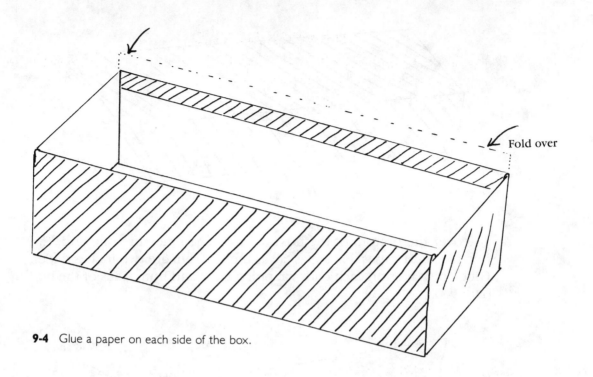

Fold over

9-4 Glue a paper on each side of the box.

SHOEBOX HOUND

The Shoebox Hound can hold pet treats, combs, brushes, or pet toys. Try designing a box to look like your own dog!

Materials List

- Shoebox
- Black, brown, white, and pink construction paper
- Scissors
- Elmer's Glue-All
- Cellophane tape
- Black marker
- Paper punch

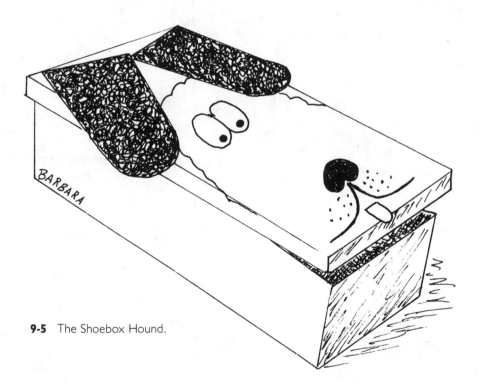

9-5 The Shoebox Hound.

Directions

1. Cover the lid of the shoebox with black paper. Cover the bottom of the box with black paper.
2. Use the patterns in FIG. 9-6 to trace and cut out a brown dog face, two black ears, a black nose, two white eyes, and a pink tongue. Use the paper punch to make two black eyeballs.

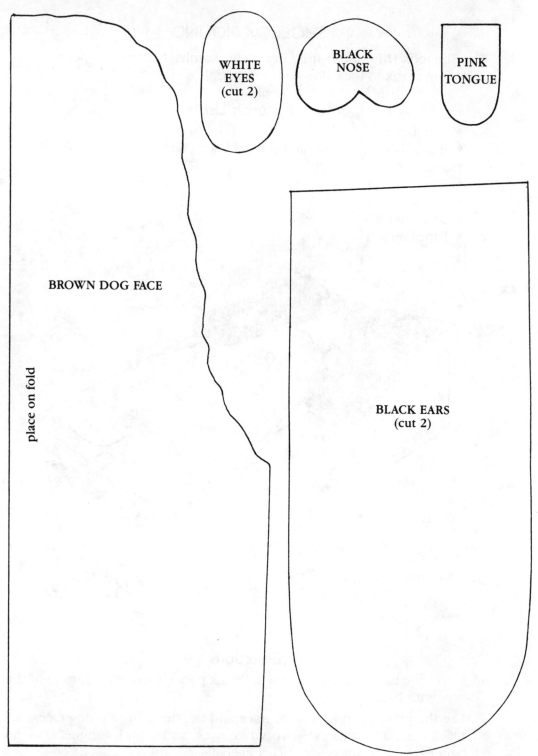

WHITE
EYES
(cut 2)

BLACK
NOSE

PINK
TONGUE

BROWN DOG FACE

place on fold

BLACK EARS
(cut 2)

9-6 The patterns for the Shoebox Hound.

3. Glue the dog face on the box lid. Glue on the white eyes and the black nose. Add the two ears.

4. Use a black marker to draw two curved lines down from the nose. Make dots with the marker to look like dog whiskers. Glue on the pink tongue.

5. Add paper-punch eyeballs.

BABY FOOD SNOW DOME

Snow domes, those shake-a-blizzard desk-top globes, are fun and easy to make with recycled baby food jars.

Materials List

- Small jar baby food
- Plastic figure that can fit in the jar (Look in a craft store for inexpensive miniatures.)
- Elmer's Stix-All Adhesive
- Toothpick to use as a tool
- 1/8 teaspoon glitter
- Sugar syrup made of 1/2 cup hot water, 2 tablespoons sugar, and 2 teaspoons light corn syrup

9-7 The Baby Food Snow Dome.

Directions

1. Eat the baby food. The fruit flavors or the puddings are delicious! Take off the jar label and wash the jar and the lid. Squirt glue in the dry lid. Set your plastic figure in the glue. Use the toothpick to smooth the glue. Pour glitter on the wet glue. Let this dry overnight.

2. Fill the baby food jar with sugar syrup. Put the lid on tightly so it will not leak. You can glue ribbon around the edge of the lid if you want to.

NOTE: Sugar and corn syrup are used to make the water thicker. This allows the glitter to fall more slowly when the Snow Dome is shaken.

woolie-pullie

To clean table and desk tops, squirt with shaving cream, rub with hands, and wipe with a sponge.

JOJO AND JOLLY CLOWN BOXES

JoJo and Jolly are made of margarine tubs topped with a white circle just like clown paint. JoJo has a pompom nose. Jolly wears a wig of Easter grass!

Materials List

- 8-ounce margarine tub for each clown box
- Pencil
- Scissors
- Black marker
- Elmer's Glue-All
- Construction paper in lots of colors
- 1/2-inch red pompom for JoJo
- Easter grass for Jolly

9-8 JoJo and Jolly Clown Boxes.

Directions

1. Take the lid off the margarine tub. Use it as a pattern to trace a circle onto white construction paper. Cut the circle out and glue it on the lid.

2. To make JoJo, use the patterns in FIG. 9-9 to trace the hair, eyes, eyeballs, mouth, and cheeks onto colored construction paper. Cut them out and glue them on the white lid.

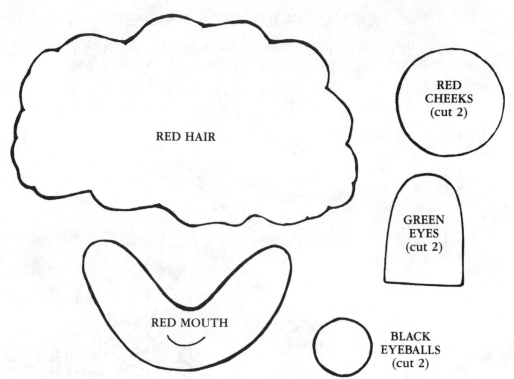

RED HAIR

RED CHEEKS
(cut 2)

GREEN EYES
(cut 2)

RED MOUTH

BLACK EYEBALLS
(cut 2)

9-9 The patterns for the JoJo Clown Box.

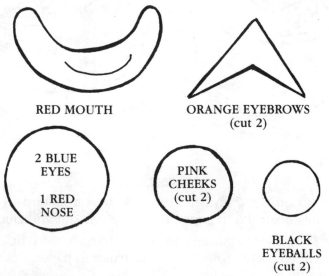

RED MOUTH

ORANGE EYEBROWS
(cut 2)

2 BLUE EYES

1 RED NOSE

PINK CHEEKS
(cut 2)

BLACK EYEBALLS
(cut 2)

9-10 The patterns for the Jolly Clown Box.

3. Add paper curls on each side of JoJo's face by cutting four strips $1/4$ by 3 inches, and wrapping the strips around a pencil. Glue one end of each curl under the edges of the clown's hair. Glue on the red pompom nose.

4. To make Jolly, use the patterns in FIG. 9-10 to trace the eyes, eyeballs, eyebrows, nose, mouth, and cheeks onto colored construction paper. Cut them out and glue them on the white lid.

5. Add an Easter grass wig by gluing as much Easter grass as you can to Jolly's head. It will look very messy and gluey, but let it dry that way. When the glue has completely dried and no longer looks white, give Jolly a haircut with scissors! Be careful not to cut yourself!

6. JoJo and Jolly Clown Boxes are perfect for holding a gift of nuts or candy. You can also use them to hold coins, jewelry, or other small treasures.

HALLOWEEN TREE

Ghosts, pumpkins, and bats hang all over a spooky tree branch! Make the Halloween Tree with a friend or two so you can tie on lots of scary creatures in less time.

9-11 The Halloween Tree.

Materials List

- Plaster of paris. (Buy this in a hardware store.)
- Coffee can
- Water
- Tree branch 24 to 30 inches high
- Orange tissue wrapping paper
- Black ribbon
- Black and orange construction paper
- White toilet tissue
- Scissors
- Elmer's Glue-All
- Narrow black marker
- Sewing needle
- Black sewing thread

Directions

1. Put the plaster of paris in the coffee can until the can is half full. Stir in water until the plaster is as thick as cake batter. Set the end of the tree branch in the can. Prop it against something sturdy until the plaster becomes firm. This takes about 20 minutes. Meanwhile, make paper pumpkins, bats, and ghosts.

2. Use the pattern in FIG. 9-12 to trace and cut out orange construction paper pumpkins and black bats. I used six of each for my branch. Make six ghosts from toilet tissue squares. First, fold a square in half twice to

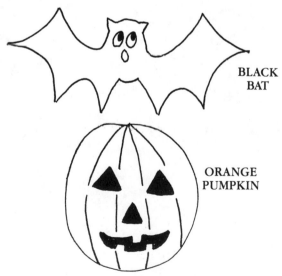

9-12 The patterns for the Halloween Tree.

make a smaller square. Pinch the square in the middle and tie black thread around the pinched part to make the ghost. Draw two eyes and a mouth on the ghost by using a narrow black marker or a pen. To make the ghost hang straight, tape the thread to the back of its head.

3. Finish the pumpkins by snipping little black triangles for the eyes and the nose and gluing them on. Draw a mouth with a black marker. Glue on a green paper stem. Put black thread in the needle. Sew through the top of each pumpkin. Tie the thread in a knot.

4. Finish the bats by adding little white paper eyes. Draw eyeballs with a marker. Use the needle and black thread to sew through the top of each bat. Tie the thread in a knot.

5. Cover the coffee can with orange tissue paper. Tie a black ribbon near the top of the can. Tie the ghosts, pumpkins, and bats all over the branch.

CYLINDER SANTA CLAUS

Any cylinder can be used to make this wonderful Santa. These measurements are for a Pringle's potato chip can.

Materials List

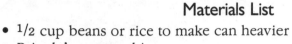

- ½ cup beans or rice to make can heavier
- Pringle's potato chip can
- Red, black, white, and green construction paper
- Ruler
- Pencil
- Scissors
- Elmer's Glue-All
- Synthetic stuffing (fiber-fill)
- ½-inch red pompom nose (Buy this in a craft store.)
- Gold foil (Look for foil wrapping paper or an old greeting card.)

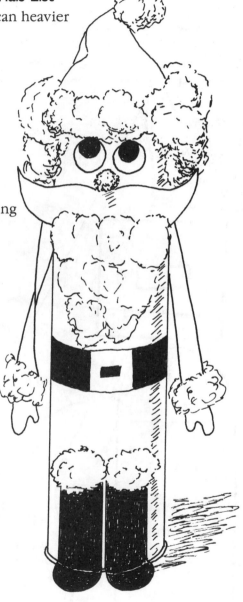

9-13 The Cylinder Santa.

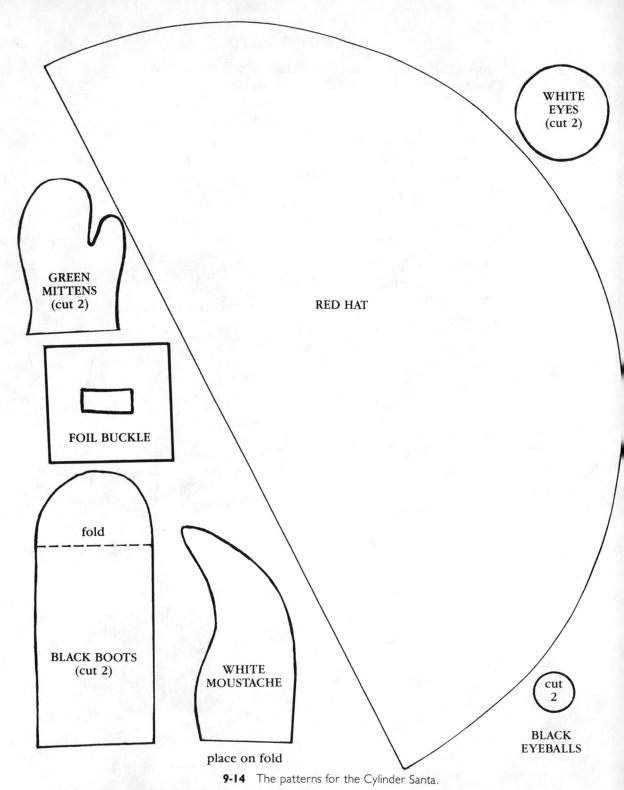

WHITE
EYES
(cut 2)

GREEN
MITTENS
(cut 2)

RED HAT

FOIL BUCKLE

fold

BLACK BOOTS
(cut 2)

WHITE
MOUSTACHE

cut
2

BLACK
EYEBALLS

place on fold

9-14 The patterns for the Cylinder Santa.

Directions

1. Put the beans or rice in the can. Put on the lid. Spread glue on a 9-by-12-inch sheet of red construction paper. Cover the can with it.

2. Use the patterns in FIG. 9-14 to trace and cut out a red hat, a white moustache, two white eyes, two black boots, two black eyeballs, two green mittens, and a gold foil belt buckle.

3. Use a ruler and pencil to measure a black belt 1 by 11 inches. Measure two red arms 1 by 5^1/2 inches. Cut these out. Pleat the arms by folding them back and forth.

4. Shape the hat into a cone that hangs over the lid a little bit. To do this, hold the hat shape with the flat edge at the top. Holding it at each

9-15 This Cylinder Santa needs a moustache, boots, and lots of cotton!

point, pull your two hands together and down. Overlap the edges until the paper comes to a sharp point at the top. Hold the cone on the can to see if it hangs over the lid a little. Glue the edges of the cone together to help it keep its shape. Squirt glue around the top of the can. Set the hat on the top.

5. Glue the white eyes and black eyeballs below the hat. Glue the pompom nose just below the eyes. Glue the white moustache below the nose.

6. Glue the arms on each side, just below the moustache. Add a mitten to the end of each arm. Glue the belt around the middle of Santa Claus. Glue on the belt buckle. Fold the boots and glue them at the bottom of the can (FIG. 9-15).

7. Squirt glue on the Santa Claus a little at a time and add cotton or stuffing to the hat, hair, beard, end of arms, and top of boots. Don't glue cotton to his moustache; he looks better without it.

10

Mostly Glue Crafts

A sticker made of Goofy Glue
Is very easy for you to do.
Just squirt glue out
And add some dye.
Cut with scissors
When it is dry!

GOOFY GLUE STICKER

A dry Goofy Glue Sticker can decorate a mirror, a television screen, or a glass window. It peels off easily. If you get the sticker wet it will stick permanently to a notebook, a book cover, or a handmade greeting card. Cut it in any shape you wish.

Materials List

- Styrofoam tray
- Plastic wrap
- Elmer's Glue-All
- Red, green, blue, and yellow liquid food dye
- 2 toothpicks
- Scissors

10-1 The Goofy Glue Sticker on stationery.

Directions

1. Turn the Styrofoam tray upside down. Cover the bottom with plastic wrap. Tuck the edges of the plastic under the tray.

2. Squirt glue on the tray to make a puddle. Use the toothpicks to spread the glue evenly over the plastic. Do not get glue too close to the edge of the tray, or it will drip off.

3. Squirt two drops of food dye in the glue. Use a toothpick to mix the color. Squirt two drops of another color of dye in the glue. Mix with a toothpick.

4. Let this dry for three days until the glue is dry and is no longer white. Peel off the plastic wrap. Use scissors to cut the Goofy Glue into shapes such as your initials, a tropical fish, or a spider.

5. Press the glossy side of your sticker against a glass window to let the sun shine through.

6. To decorate a greeting card or a book cover, wet the sticker on one side. Press the wet side onto the card. Let it dry.

CEREAL ADVENT WREATH

The word *advent* means *to come into place.* An Advent wreath has four candles to mark the four Sundays before Christmas. This wreath is made of crushed shredded wheat cereal!

Materials List

- Posterboard
- Pencil
- Scissors
- 1/2 cup shredded wheat cereal (14 bite-sized mini-wheats)
- Plastic cup
- Popsicle stick for stirring
- 2 teaspoons Elmer's Glue-All
- Green food dye
- 4 birthday candles
- Red construction paper
- Paper punch

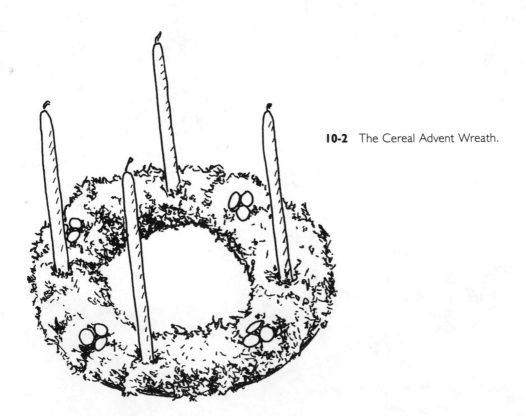

10-2 The Cereal Advent Wreath.

Directions

1. Use the pattern in FIG. 10-3 to trace and cut out a posterboard wreath.

2. Crush the cereal with your fingers and put it in the plastic cup. Add two teaspoons of Elmer's Glue-All and a squirt of green food dye. Stir this mixture with a popsicle stick until it is all green. Spread glue on the posterboard wreath.

3. Use the popsicle stick to pile the green cereal evenly on the posterboard. Don't use your fingers because this is too sticky!

4. Dip the bottom of each candle in glue. Stick the candles in the cereal wreath. Use the paper punch and red paper to make 12 holly berries. Glue these between the candles in groups of three. Let your Cereal Advent Wreath dry overnight.

woolie-pullie

To make Cereal Advent Wreaths with 24 children, use a 1 1/2-pound box of bite-sized shredded wheat cereal.

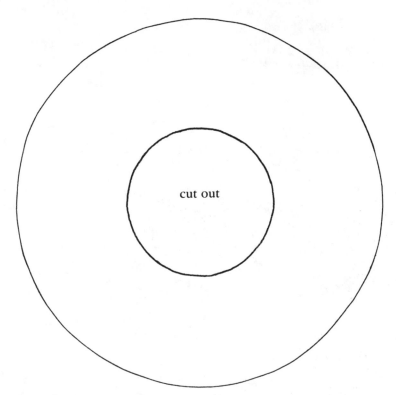

cut out

10-3 The pattern for the Cereal Advent Wreath.

II

Posterboard Projects

An eagle flaps
Its beautiful wings
As if it could fly away.
A butterfly holds
A note in its mouth;
Perhaps your thought for the day.

AMERICAN EAGLE

The bald eagle has been the national bird of the United States since 1782. It lives only in North America. This American Eagle craft can be decorated with red, white, and blue stripes plus stars. It can also be colored to look like Army camouflage.

Materials List

- Posterboard
- Markers or crayons
- Scissors
- Elmer's Glue-All
- Stars (optional)

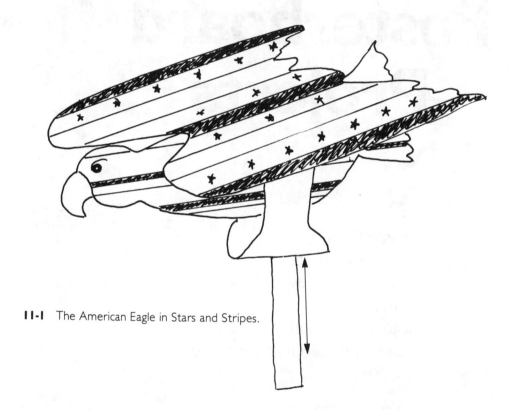

11-1 The American Eagle in Stars and Stripes.

1. Use the four patterns (FIGS. 11-2, 11-3, 11-4) to trace the body, wings, midsection, and the stick onto cardboard. Cut them out. Color the four pieces with crayons to look like Army camouflage or use red, white, and blue to resemble our American flag. If you like, you can add stars too.

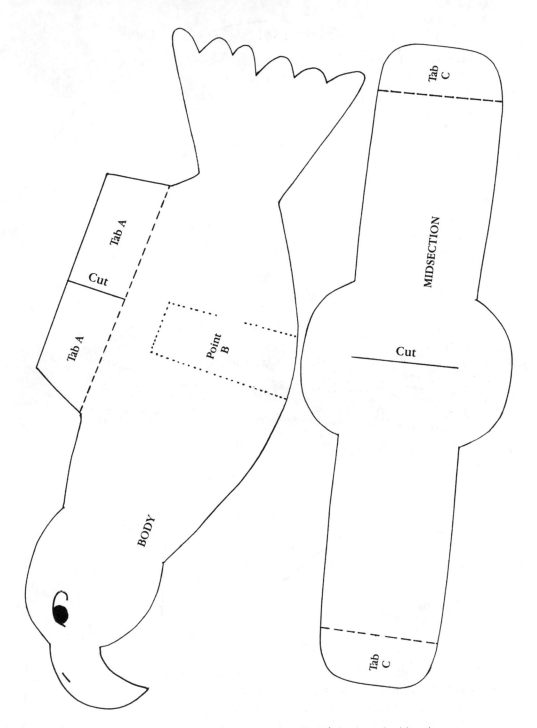

Tab A

Cut

Tab A

Point B

BODY

Tab C

MIDSECTION

Cut

Tab C

11-2 The patterns for the American Eagle's body and midsection.

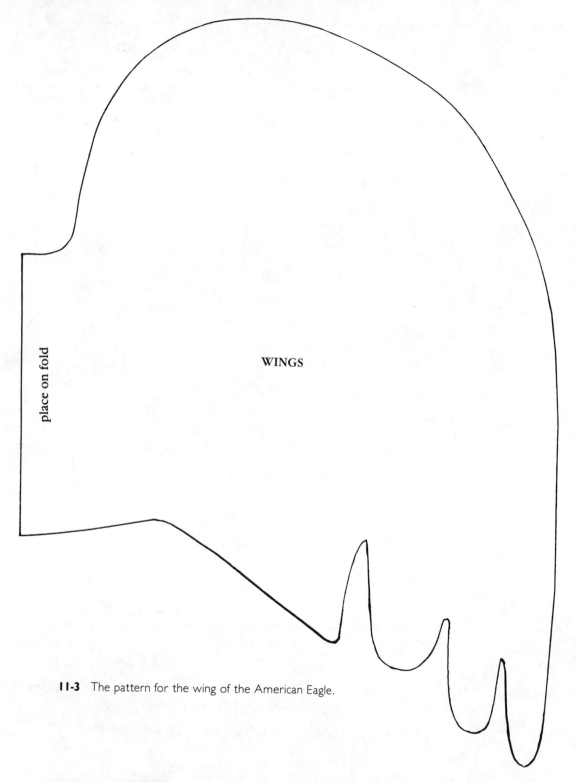

place on fold

WINGS

11-3 The pattern for the wing of the American Eagle.

	Tab B
	cut
fold	
THE STICK	Tab B

11-4 The pattern for the stick of the American Eagle.

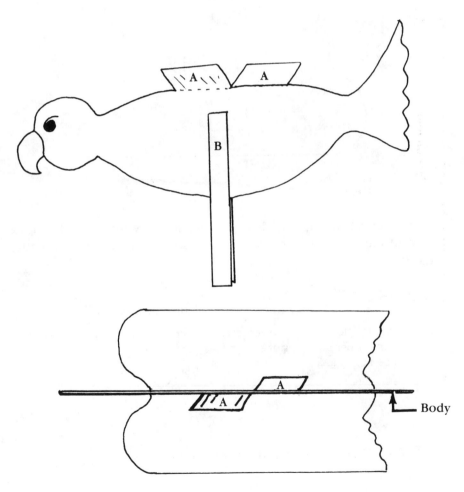

11-5 Glue the body in the middle of the wing.

2. Fasten the body to the wings by putting the glue on Tabs A of the body. Glue the body in the middle of the wings (FIG. 11-5).

3. Fold the stick in half on the dotted line. The stick has been cut 3/4 inches to make Tabs B. Put glue on Tabs B and glue the stick on both sides of the body at point B. Glue the stick shut.

4. You have made a cut in the midsection. Push the end of the stick through this cut. Push the midsection up to the eagle's body as far as it will go. Glue Tabs C to the wings (FIG. 11-6).

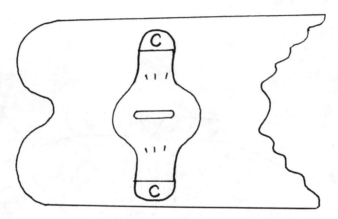

11-6 Glue Tabs C to the underside of the wing.

5. Let the eagle dry upside down. To make the wings flap, hold the stick in one hand and move the midsection up and down with the other hand.

woolie-pullie

Use a ruler to fold paper or posterboard. Lay the ruler on the line that you want to fold. Lift the paper up against the ruler. Press it over the ruler with your fingers. The fold will be neat and fast.

BUTTERFLY NOTE CLIP

A magnet on the back of the Butterfly Note Clip lets you hang it on any metal surface. Use it to hold a recipe, a note, or a prayer.

Materials List

- Posterboard
- Pencil
- Scissors
- Set of markers
- Ruler
- Clip clothespin
- Elmer's Glue-All
- Paper punch
- Strip magnet 3 inches long (Buy this in a craft store.)

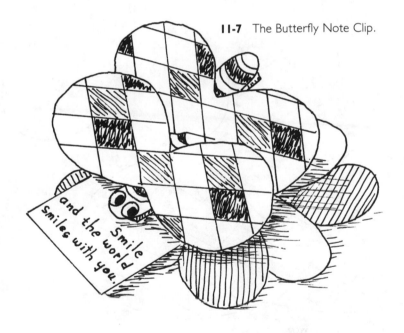

11-7 The Butterfly Note Clip.

Directions

1. Use the patterns in FIG. 11-8 to trace a flower, a butterfly body, and two wings onto posterboard. Cut these out.
2. Color the flower with markers. Glue the clothespin on the flower (FIG. 11-9). Color the body and glue it on the clothespin.

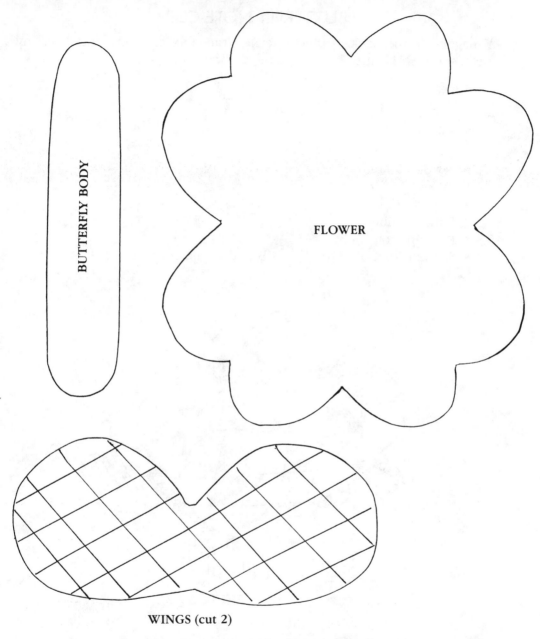

BUTTERFLY BODY

FLOWER

WINGS (cut 2)

11-8 The patterns for the Butterfly Note Clip.

3. Use the ruler and pencil to draw squares and rectangles on the wings. Color these with bright markers. Bend the wings up in the middle. Glue them to the butterfly body, one behind the other.

11-9 Glue the clothespin on the flower.

4. Glue on two paper-punch eyes. Draw eyeballs with a dark marker. Cut a strip magnet 3 inches long and stick it to the bottom of the flower. Squeeze the clothespin to open it and stick a note in the butterfly's mouth.

_____ **woolie-pullie** _____

Use a pencil to flatten a fold in the posterboard. Just lay the pencil on its side and smooth it firmly back and forth over the folded edge.

12

Cooking Crafts

In this final chapter
Get out a bowl and spoon.
If it's praise you're after,
Cook these things real soon!
One of the foods looks funny,
Shaped like a pig;
Some are gooey and crunchy.
But they'll all go over BIG!

PIGGY PIZZAS

Piggy, Piggy Pizzas! Give three cheers for the pepperoni nose and the tortilla ears!

Materials List

- 6 English muffins
- 1 cup spaghetti sauce
- 8 ounces shredded mozzarella cheese
- 12 pepperoni slices
- 12 pitted black olives
- 12 green olives with pimentos
- 24 triangle-shaped tortilla snack chips
- Cookie sheet

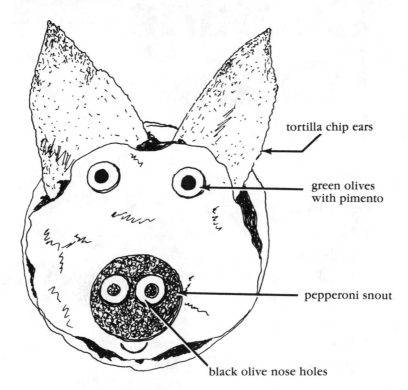

tortilla chip ears

green olives with pimento

pepperoni snout

black olive nose holes

12-1 A Piggy Pizza.

Directions

1. Cut the muffins in half. Lay them on the cookie sheet, cut-side up. An adult can help you toast them in the oven until they are light brown and crisp. Don't forget to use a potholder so you won't burn yourself.

2. Spread a spoonful of spaghetti sauce on each muffin. Put cheese on each one.

3. Look at the picture. Make a pig face on each muffin. Make a pepperoni snout. Add two black olive slices for nose holes. Make eyes from a green olive cut in two. Stick two tortilla chips in the cheese at the top of the head to make ears.

4. Bake the Piggy Pizzas in a 350°F oven for 10 minutes, or until the cheese melts. If the ears fall over, set them back up after baking. The cheese will hold them up as it cools.

woolie-pullie

Turn a paper plate into a pouch to carry cooking crafts. Fold the plate in half with the cooking craft inside. Tape or staple it closed. Write your name on it.

GRAHAM POPPERS

Add raisins, nuts, or chocolate chips to these treats. When you chill them they become tender-crisp!

Materials List

- Pot for the stove, or bowl for the microwave
- Wooden spoon
- 6 large marshmallows
- 1 cup smooth peanut butter
- $1/2$ cup raisins or chopped nuts or chocolate chips
- 1 cup graham cracker crumbs

Directions

1. Put the marshmallows and the peanut butter in a pot; stir together. Ask an adult to help you at the stove. Cook over low heat until the marshmallows melt. MICROWAVE DIRECTIONS: Put the marshmallows and peanut butter in a microwave bowl. Microwave on HIGH for 2 minutes, then stir well.

2. Add the raisins or nuts or chocolate chips. Add the graham cracker crumbs. Stir the Graham Poppers until everything is mixed together into a dough.

3 Shape the Graham Poppers into balls as big as a walnut. Eat them right away or put them in the refrigerator. In 30 minutes they will become tender-crisp.

HIGH ENERGY HIKING BARS

For a yummy snack, pack these High Energy Hiking Bars in your backpack or your school lunch box. You can add other goodies to this recipe, such as chocolate chips and marshmallows!

Materials List

- Pot for the stove
- Large bowl
- Wooden spoon
- 1$\frac{1}{2}$ cups peanut butter
- 1 cup honey or light corn syrup
- $\frac{3}{4}$ cup brown sugar
- 6 cups whole-grain cereal such as Raisin Bran
- $\frac{1}{2}$ cup raisins
- 1 cup coconut
- 9-by-13-inch pan
- Margarine to grease pan

Directions

1. Measure the peanut butter, honey or corn syrup, and brown sugar into the pot. Stir over medium heat until the mixture is smooth and bubbly. (Have an adult help you at the stove.) Pour into the bowl.

2. Add the cereal, raisins, and coconut. Stir well. Grease the pan with margarine. Pour the Hiking Bar mixture into the pan.

3. Press the mixture into the pan as hard as you can with the heel of your hand. Cover it with plastic wrap, and set it aside for an hour. Cut it into bars and wrap for a hiking trip, or eat right away.

CHOCOLATE PEANUT BUTTER CREAMS

Use a microwave or stove to melt chocolate chips in Chocolate Peanut Butter Creams. These are easy to make, and oh so yummy!

Materials List
- Pot for the stove or bowl for the microwave
- Wooden spoon
- 6 ounces chocolate chips
- 14-ounce can sweetened condensed milk
- 1 3/4 cups creamy peanut butter
- 1/2 cup powdered sugar

Directions
1. Measure the chocolate chips, sweetened condensed milk, and peanut butter into a pot. Ask permission to stir and cook over low heat until the chocolate chips melt. MICROWAVE DIRECTIONS: Measure the three ingredients into a microwave bowl. Microwave on HIGH for two minutes, then stir well.

2. Add the powdered sugar. Stir until the mixture is smooth.

3. You can roll the creams into balls or into any other shapes you like. Put them in the refrigerator to make them harder.

CHOCOLATE RAISIN BARS

Chocolate Raisin Bars can be cooked on the stove, on a hot plate, or in a microwave oven. Slip plastic sandwich bags on your hands to press them into the pan. Mmmm, are they good!

Materials List

- Pot for the stove, or bowl for the microwave
- Wooden spoon
- 1/2 cup milk
- 1/2 cup light corn syrup
- 1 cup raisins
- 2 tablespoons margarine
- 6 ounces chocolate chips
- 5 cups crispy rice cereal
- 1 cup miniature marshmallows
- 9-inch square pan, greased

Directions

1. Measure the milk, corn syrup, raisins, margarine, and chocolate chips into a pot. Ask an adult to help you cook the mixture over low heat until everything melts. Simmer this mixture for four minutes, stirring constantly. Remove from the heat. MICROWAVE DIRECTIONS: Measure the five ingredients into the microwave bowl. Microwave on HIGH for four minutes. Stir until the mixture is smooth. Microwave for four minutes more. Stir again.

2. Add 5 cups of crispy rice cereal and 1 cup of marshmallows. Stir together well. Pour the batter into the greased pan. Press it into the pan with your hands. You can butter your hands to do this, or you can use plastic sandwich bags as "gloves."

3. Refrigerate the Chocolate Raisin Bars for one hour. Cut them into 24 pieces.

Index

Other Bestsellers of Related Interest

SHARING TIME: A Big Person/Little Person Project Book—Kathy Leichliter Miller

Forty creative answers to "What can I do?" are contained in this book. An ideal resource for parents, elementary school teachers, babysitters, and daycare operators, *Sharing Time* offers inexpensive, fun-filled, and educational projects for adults and children to make together. Each project features step-by-step illustrations, complete materials lists, and easy-to-follow instructions. Book No. 3256, $12.95 paperback only

SCIENCE FOR KIDS: 39 Easy Astronomy Experiments—Robert W. Wood

While learning about the wonders of the sky, kids will classify stars by temperature, use refracting and reflecting telescopes, photograph star tracks, and much more. 154 pages, illustrated. Book No. 3597, $9.95 paperback, $17.95 hardcover

PHYSICS FOR KIDS: 49 Easy Experiments with Electricity and Magnetism—Robert W. Wood

What makes a magnet stick to the refrigerator? What makes the batteries in a flashlight work? Find the answers to these questions, and more, in this entertaining and instructional project book. These quick, safe, and inexpensive experiments include making items like: a magnet, potato battery, flashlight, compass, telegraph, model railroad signal, and electric lock. 142 pages, 151 illustrations. Book No. 3412, $9.95 paperback, $16.95 hardcover

SCIENCE MAGIC FOR KIDS: 68 Simple & Safe Experiments—William R. Wellnitz, Ph.D.

An understanding and appreciation of science by youngsters in grades K-5 requires active, hands-on participation. Wellnitz provides dozens of simple projects that help children discover the "magic" of science, learning basic scientific principles as they play with safe and inexpensive materials commonly found around the house. Projects include the chemistry of color, food and nutrition, properties of soap bubbles, and general biology. 128 pages, 102 illustrations. Book No. 3423, $9.95 paperback only

CRAFTS FOR KIDS: A Month-By-Month Idea Book—2nd Edition—Barbara L. Dondiego; Illustrations by Jacqueline Cawley

Packed with dozens of inexpensive project ideas, this book is perfect for busy parents, teachers, and youth leaders looking for ideas. With just a little help from you, children ages two and up can make watercolor paintings, paper-punch valentines, pinecone owls, clothespin dolls, cherry refrigerator magnets, no-cook peanut butter balls, juice-can animals, and many other items guaranteed to keep them busy. 240 pages, 164 illustrations. Book No. 3573, $14.95 paperback only

YEAR-ROUND CRAFTS FOR KIDS—Barabara L. Dondiego, Illustrated by Jacqueline Cawley

Easy to use, the handy month-by-month format provides a year of inspiring projects, many focused on seasonal themes to ensure young children's enthusiasm. Valentines, paper airplanes, and cookies for Easter, paper bag bunny puppets, string painting, Hanukkah candles and gingerbread boys, bell and candle mobiles and of course Christmas trees for December are just a few of the fun things to make. 256 pages, 180 illustrations. Book No. 2904, $12.95 paperback only

"I MADE IT MYSELF": 40 Kids' Crafts Projects—Alan and Gill Bridgewater

This easy project book will give children hours of fun crafting toys and gifts with inexpensive household materials. Children will enjoy making musical instruments, kites, dolls, cards, masks, papier-mâché and painted ornaments, as well as working toys such as a wind racer, land yacht, or moon buggy. Along with easy-to-follow instructions, each project includes scale drawings, step-by-step illustrations, and a picture of the finished item. 224 pages, 165 illustrations. Book No. 3339, $11.95 paperback only

Look for These and Other TAB Books at Your Local Bookstore

To Order Call Toll Free 1-800-822-8158

or write to TAB Books, Blue Ridge Summit, PA 17294-0840.

Title	Product No.	Quantity	Price

☐ Check or money order made payable to TAB Books

Charge my ☐ VISA ☐ MasterCard ☐ American Express

Acct. No. _____ Exp. _____

Signature: _____

Name: _____

Address: _____

City: _____

State: _____ Zip: _____

Subtotal $ _____

Postage and Handling
($3.00 in U.S., $5.00 outside U.S.) $ _____

Add applicable state and local
sales tax $ _____

TOTAL $ _____

TAB Books catalog free with purchase; otherwise send $1.00 in check or money order and receive $1.00 credit on your next purchase.

Orders outside U.S. must pay with international money in U.S. dollars

TAB Guarantee: If for any reason you are not satisfied with the book(s) you order, simply return it (them) within 15 days and receive a full refund. BC